Helping Others Receive the *GIFT*

Joshua 1:9

Helping Others Receive the *G*IFT

Insights on Spirit Baptism from God's Word and Personal Experience

Compiled and Edited by
TIM ENLOE

Foreword by
RANDY HURST

ACCESS

©2008 The Access Group

All scripture quotations, unless otherwise indicated,
are taken from the *Holy Bible, New International Version*®. NIV®.
Copyright ©1973, 1978, 1984 by International Bible Society.
Used by permission of Zondervan. All rights reserved.

KJV indicates the King James Version of the Bible.

Scripture quotations marked (NASB®) are taken from the
New American Standard Bible®, Copyright © 1960, 1962, 1963, 1968,
1971, 1972, 1973, 1975, 1977, 1995 by The Lockman Foundation.
Used by permission. (www.Lockman.org)

Contents

Foreword 11

Chapter One 15
THE NUTS AND BOLTS OF MINISTERING SPIRIT BAPTISM
By Tim Enloe

Chapter Two 29
CONFESSIONS OF A CHRONIC SEEKER
By Randy Hurst

Chapter Three 41
PREPARING YOURSELF TO HELP OTHERS
By Ken Cramer

Chapter Four 49
MINISTERING THE HOLY SPIRIT BAPTISM IN TODAY'S CULTURE
By Gary Grogan

Chapter Five 55
PARTNERING WITH SEEKERS
By Judi Bullock

Chapter Six 63
FOSTERING A SETTING FOR PEOPLE TO RECEIVE
By Scott Erickson

Chapter Seven 71
ENCOURAGEMENT IN RECEIVING THE GIFT
By Bill Juoni

Chapter Eight 77
THE HOLY SPIRIT AND SMALL GROUPS
By Randy Valimont

Chapter Nine 85
LEADING A RECEIVING TIME
By Tim Enloe with others

CHILDREN'S MINISTRY

Chapter Ten 93
THE HOLY SPIRIT BAPTISM AND CHILDREN
By Dick Gruber

Chapter Eleven 105
COMMUNICATING THE CHARACTER OF THE HOLY SPIRIT TO KIDS
By Jim Gerhold

YOUTH MINISTRY

Chapter Twelve 113
COMMUNICATING THE BAPTISM IN THE HOLY SPIRIT TO STUDENTS
By Allen Griffin

Chapter Thirteen 123
PREPARING A LEADERSHIP TEAM
By Nate Ruch

THEOLOGICAL PERSPECTIVES

Chapter Fourteen 133
THEOLOGICAL, HISTORICAL, AND PRACTICAL INSIGHTS ON SPIRIT BAPTISM
By Dr. Gordon Anderson

Chapter Fifteen 149
A LINGUIST LOOKS AT THE MYSTERY OF TONGUES
By Dr. Del Tarr

Contributors

Dr. Gordon Anderson has written frequently and spoken at many conventions with regard to Pentecostal issues. He has been active in Assemblies of God higher education for the past twenty-five years, including serving as the director of education for Eurasia from 1992 to 1995 and president of North Central University from 1995 to present. www.northcentral.edu

Judi Bullock has served with her husband, Warren, as pastor of four churches as well as superintendent of the Northwest District. They are currently pastoring the Northwest Family Church in Auburn, Washington, where she is Women's Ministries Director.

Ken Cramer and his wife, Holly, have a mandate from God on their lives to raise up one hundred sons and daughters for fulltime ministry. They are accomplishing this through the ministry of Lighthouse Worship Center in Gloucester, Virginia, where they serve as senior pastors. www.lighthouseworshipcenter.com

Tim Enloe, and his wife, Rochelle, conduct Holy Spirit conferences which emphasize a practical, nonmystical approach to the Holy Spirit's power and giftings. Many people experience salvation, the baptism in the Holy Spirit and healing as the Enloes minister in song, teaching, and during extended times of seeking God around the altars. www.enloeministries.org

Scott Erickson has served as senior pastor of the Peoples Church in Salem, Oregon since 2000. He also serves as an executive presbyter for the Oregon District and has been involved in crusades and leadership training in forty-eight nations. www.peopleschurch.com

Jim Gerhold has served as a children's pastor for most of his ministry as well the children's ministries coordinator for the Assemblies of God. He is currently on staff at Park Crest Assembly in Springfield, Missouri. www.kidnique.com

Allen Griffin has been ministering as an itinerant revivalist and evangelist throughout the United States and internationally for fourteen years. Allen and his wife, Hashmareen, have two sons and reside in Daytona Beach, Florida. www.AGMinistries.com

Gary Grogan has been lead pastor of Urbana Assembly in Urbana, Illinois since 1988 and has seen the church grow from fifty people to a weekly average of 1,200 in five Sunday morning services. The church has planted four churches and sent people to revitalize another. www.urbanaassembly.org

Dick Gruber has served in leadership in children's ministries since March 1975. Since June of 2001, he has served as the children's ministries specialist at Valley Forge Christian College. www.dickgruber.com or www.cmuniversity.org

Randy Hurst is Assemblies of God commissioner of evangelism and communications director for Assemblies of God World Missions. He is a missionary evangelist, and has also authored a number of books, as well as articles in *Today's Pentecostal Evangel*.

Bill Juoni served as an Assemblies of God senior pastor for twenty years, prior to being called to the ministry of an evangelist. He presently serves on the National Evangelists Committee and as the district evangelists representative for the Wisconsin/Northern Michigan District.

Nate Ruch served as a youth pastor from 1994 to 2003. He currently serves as the co-director for the Center for Youth and Leadership at North Central University. He speaks in youth camps, conventions, and district youth pastor retreats as well as teaching youth ministry students at NCU. www.northcentral.edu or www.youthandleadership.com

Dr. Del Tarr served as president of Assemblies of God Theological Seminary from 1990 to 1999. He and his wife, Dolly, continue to minister around the world as specially appointed missionaries, spending five to six months a year overseas at AG graduate institutions.

Randy Valimont has pastored at First Assembly of God in Griffin, Georgia, since 1993. Since then, the church has grown from four hundred to more than 3,500. Randy is currently an executive presbyter of the Georgia District and general presbyter for the General Council. www.griffinfirst.org

FOREWORD

Pentecostals are at a critical crossroads concerning the Holy Spirit baptism. At the heart of the issue are these three questions regarding Spirit baptism which we simply refer to as "the gift":

> Has the gift made a difference?
> Is the gift worth it?
> Is the gift essential?

The authors of this book believe the answer to all three questions is yes.

First, has Spirit baptism made a difference in the effectiveness of the mission of the Assemblies of God? Any thoughtful examination of our history reveals that the empowerment of the Spirit is an intrinsic factor in what has been accomplished both through the U.S. church and through our missionaries and fraternal fellowships around the world

Second, do the spiritual benefits that accompany Spirit baptism outweigh the extremes, abuses, and embarrassment that have been associated with some Pentecostal practices in the past—especially concerning the manifestation of spiritual gifts? This issue is of vital concern and must be clearly and comprehensively addressed as ministers intentionally encourage people to seek for Spirit baptism. This issue is addressed in *Divine Order*, which is being released simultaneously with this book, and in the "Spiritual Gifts" section of the evangelism commission's Web site: HolySpirit.ag.org.

Third, is Spirit baptism essential or merely beneficial to Christian life and service? The simplest and clearest answer to this question is found in Jesus' instructions to His first disciples. Our Master's last words recorded by Luke are these: "That repentance for forgiveness of sins would be proclaimed in His name to all the nations, beginning from Jerusalem. You are witnesses of these things. And behold, I am sending forth the promise of My Father upon you; but you are to stay in the city until you are clothed with power from on high" (Luke 24:47–49, NASB).

It would seem that a task as great as proclaiming Christ's message to all the nations should commence immediately. But Jesus told the disciples to wait in the city to be "clothed with power from on high."

American Express ran a successful ad campaign that depicted a person on a trip without the necessary resources. The theme was "Don't leave home without it!" Jesus was telling His disciples essentially the same thing—that they should not begin their mission without being equipped to accomplish the task. He clearly implied that the fullness of the Spirit is essential to fulfilling the purposes and mission to which He has called us.

Soon after the Commission on Evangelism was formed by the Executive and General Presbyteries, we sent a survey to pastors in the Fellowship to ascertain what aspects of evangelism they most wanted resources for local church ministry. From the more than one thousand surveys returned, resources concerning Spirit baptism were among the three most requested topics.

We began production of a video featuring commission members in a roundtable discussion on the purpose and importance of the Holy Spirit baptism. Then-General Superintendent Thomas Trask saw the first draft of the video and asked us to make a DVD available to every pastor. The *Power for Purpose* DVD was distributed nationwide, and hundreds of pastors responded regarding its effectiveness. Each year since then, the Evangelism Commission has been asked by our leadership to produce resources for an annual Holy Spirit emphasis.

Testimonies from those who use these resources are inspiring. As pastors have brought attention and understanding to the person and work of the Spirit, thousands of people—even hundreds in individual churches—have received the gift of Spirit baptism in just a few weeks' time. If we seek Jesus—the Baptizer—in faith, He *will* baptize and keep refilling us with the Spirit's presence and power!

This book is another resource we pray will bless congregations. I believe it is both unique and unprecedented. Those who are helped by this book owe a special debt of gratitude to evangelist Tim Enloe who conceived the project and brought together the contributing authors. The touch of the Spirit is on Tim's ministry in churches, conferences, and also on this project.

This book was designed to give practical help to pastors, evangelists, missionaries, youth pastors, and children's pastors as they do what the title states—help others receive the gift of Spirit baptism. It will also be instructive to students preparing for ministry.

You will find some repetition in the chapters. This is intentional. When writers emphasized similar aspects of seeking and receiving the Spirit's fullness, certain points needed to be repeated to emphasize their importance and priority.

The book consists of four sections, the first of which is general instruction. The authors of this section—Tim Enloe, Ken Cramer, Gary Grogan, Judi Bullock, Scott Erickson, Bill Juoni, and Randy Valimont—contributed a wide variety of insights and observations for everyone who desires to help others receive the gift of Spirit baptism.

The second section is directed especially to those working with children. From the beginning of our Fellowship, children have been encouraged to seek Spirit baptism even at an early age. Sunday School teachers, children's pastors, and Royal Rangers and Girls Ministries leaders will all benefit from the practical teaching Dick Gruber and Jim Gerhold provide.

The third section, written by Allen Griffin and Nate Ruch, is directed to those working with youth. More than at any time in our history, youth are facing challenges for which the empowerment of the Spirit is essential to effective Christian living and preparing for the future.

The authors of the fourth section are two highly respected educators and scholars, Gordon Anderson and Del Tarr. They offer invaluable instruction not only to educators, but also to anyone in ministry. Their chapters will help assess the three questions given at the beginning of this foreword. Gordon Anderson's perspectives provide a wide variety of insights concerning theological, historical, and practical issues relating to Spirit baptism. Del Tarr's contribution is a condensed version of a chapter for a book he is writing. His insights concerning tongues and praying in the Spirit are some of the finest original thinking on the subject I've ever read.

I am certain that the insights and wisdom shared in this book will be both theologically and practically helpful to you. Each author wrote from many years of study in God's Word and practical ministry experience. Each is passionate about seeing people experience the Spirit's fullness. Those who contributed to this project are praying it will result in increasing effectiveness when instructing and praying with people as they seek the wonderful gift of the Spirit's fullness—not just initially, but also as an ongoing practice of living in the Spirit.

—RANDY HURST
Assemblies of God Commissioner of Evangelism,
Communications Director of AG World Missions

CHAPTER ONE

THE NUTS AND BOLTS OF MINISTERING SPIRIT BAPTISM

By Tim Enloe

My wife, Rochelle, and I have traveled in teaching ministry for almost fifteen years. Our emphasis is the Holy Spirit and His work, most specifically, leading people to understand and receive Spirit baptism. During these years, we have consistently encountered pastors who are personally discouraged with preaching or teaching on this subject—let alone actually praying with someone to receive the Baptism. On more than one occasion, even long-tenured senior pastors have confided that they have never successfully led someone into Spirit baptism.

The unfortunate but well-trodden path seems to follow a course like this. At some point, the minister addresses the subject with limited positive response. From that moment forward, this perceived lack of response dictates how the pastor views his or her own ability to minister on Spirit baptism. The next time the topic comes up, the minister often approaches it from a "spiritual risk management" perspective: "How can I talk about this without making those who don't receive feel badly—and how can I get through this without feeling even more unproductive myself?" That person's teaching on the Baptism begins to describe the experience as optional or, in some more unfortunate cases, as an unusual, atypical experience. It morphs from a basic step in Christian discipleship into a spiritual aftermarket accessory—or even the apologetic excuse for some people's untimely outbursts in church services.

How can something that is supposed to increase the vitality and effectiveness of the church come to be viewed as a source of frustration—or even a liability? I believe that part of the problem is misconceptions. Just a few simple misunderstandings about Spirit baptism can actually eliminate this experience from the priorities of a minister and, therefore, the life of a church.

In our many conversations with pastors, the same simple misconceptions seem to surface. These misconceptions are what we'll look at first. Then we'll move on to the actual biblical process of ministering and receiving this gift—where we'll encounter the "nuts and bolts."

MISCONCEPTIONS

Misconception #1: *When*

This first basic misconception greatly hinders ministering Spirit baptism and has to do with chronology. When should a believer seek to receive the Baptism? Isn't it for the well-worn veteran? After all, something with so much potential baggage surely can't be handled by a fragile new convert!

The church in America struggles with discipleship and assimilation. We want results similar to the Book of Acts, but we refuse to implement the clearly stated apostolic discipleship model. How can we expect Acts-like results when we reject Acts-like processes?

The two basic steps of apostolic discipleship in Acts are (1) water baptism and (2) Spirit baptism; then teaching and fellowship would follow. Jesus established this model; He told the newly born-again believers to put life on hold until they had received this gift (Luke 24:49; Acts 1:4–8). The first Pentecostal outpouring was so strongly marked by this model that it affected the preaching of that day. Peter's sermon thesis to the unbelievers was essentially: "If you want to receive the promise of the Holy Spirit, you need to get saved and baptized in water first" (Acts 2:38,39). We see the

Samaritan revival in Acts 8 and the Gentile revivals in Acts 10 and 19 following the same discipleship model.

The apostle Paul admits he was intentional in putting supernatural ministry before teaching because he didn't want the Corinthians' faith to rest on the wisdom of men, but rather on God's power (1 Corinthians 2:4,5). Paul went on to say that he did speak a message of wisdom (teaching), but it was to the mature—not to the beginner.

Why did they embrace such a seemingly volatile and risky model? The answer is simple. It was the same model under which they were discipled. Just ask Paul, whose life was altered following an epiphany on the Damascus interstate. Jesus prompted Ananias to begin Paul's discipleship the same way (Acts 9:17,18).

Please don't misunderstand me; I believe in teaching—after all, I am a teacher by calling. But I am convinced teaching finds a deeper resting place in the hearts of those who have spiritual experience.

A major reason why many avoid the apostolic discipleship pattern has to do with another misconception.

Misconception #2: Why

When it comes to understanding the "why" of Spirit baptism, I believe a major roadblock is built out of obsessively focusing on tongues-speaking rather than the true purpose of the gift. Why do we need to be Spirit baptized? Is the centerpiece really tongues?

I have heard sermons that are supposed to enable and encourage people to receive Spirit baptism digress into arguments over Greek verbs. While the substance of the arguments is true, the audience can easily misinterpret Spirit baptism as supplying "power to fight" rather than "power to witness." The purpose and practice of the Pentecostal reality is sidelined while the theologians brain-wrestle. Many pastors may feel too frustrated to bother entering this arena—especially when they still have two funerals and a wedding before they can find time to study for Sunday's sermon. The layperson must sit back wondering why they should even desire to receive the Baptism in the Spirit if all they have heard is tongues issues and impractical arguments.

I frequently ask leaders, "Why would someone want to receive Spirit baptism?" The typical answer is, "So they can speak in tongues and have a prayer language." Somehow we have lost the simple purity of Pentecost. Suddenly the focus is an argument that we have to win rather than a gateway to Spirit-empowered ministry. The sad reality is that when many ministers see an inkblot of a dove, the first thing that enters their minds is tongues.

I am firmly convinced the first outward sign (or initial evidence) of Spirit baptism is speaking in unlearned languages (or tongues). But the reason I am convinced of this is not because it is a foundational truth of the Assemblies of God; rather, Spirit baptism has a specific, obvious, biblical function. "Function" is the key word, not "argument." Our present culture has little tolerance for dogmatic religious types standing on soapboxes; people want practical truth they can personally engage and implement. The good news is Spirit baptism is such a truth, easy to understand and utilize.

The first two or three years of our ministry saw very few people actually receiving Spirit baptism. I was so frustrated. After all, that is what our ministry was supposed to target, yet there seemed to be some kind of barrier. After a few days of frustration and prayer, fasting and introspection, the Holy Spirit began to show me I was approaching this blessing with an argument. I began to reevaluate my approach alongside the Book of Acts, particularly the second chapter. Suddenly, the lightbulb turned on! I began to see that the *why* was functional in ways I had never previously understood.

On the Day of Pentecost, they were all filled and began to speak in unlearned languages as the Spirit empowered them. They began to speak out God-inspired words in another language as the Spirit enabled them. Then, some time afterwards, a group of people gathering for the feast heard them. They had two basic responses. Some were amazed and some thought this noisy bunch was drunk. That's where Act 2:14 comes in. Peter stops speaking to God in his unlearned, spiritual language and begins to address the gathered crowd—probably in Aramaic or Hebrew, preaching a most convincing and well-ordered sermon. His content was obviously beyond his natural ability.

This is where the utilitarian function of tongues helps us understand precisely *why* we need Spirit baptism: If you can trust God to order your words in the spiritual language, how much more can you trust Him to order your words in your own language to unbelievers? Spirit baptism is about saying the right things: first, the God-inspired tongues, but also in our known languages, as we prophetically minister words from God's heart.

Since the day I began to understand Acts 2, I've never had to argue the initial, physical evidence of tongues with anyone. Biblically, tongues is a prophetic confirmation of a prophetic anointing to be a prophetic witness. That's why Peter explained the event as the fulfillment of Joel's oracle where one day everyone could be a prophet.

Suddenly, speaking in tongues takes on a vital, functional role for the believer who wants to be a prophetic witness. Why do we need Spirit baptism? It's all about God affecting what we say—plain and simple.

We need Spirit baptism not primarily so we can speak in tongues; we need it so we can speak to lost people. We also receive the added benefit of communing with God in a new language.

I often encounter people who say, "I've received Spirit baptism, but haven't received the gift of tongues." The wording of such a statement makes it obvious they need some clarity. But, if my response begins with correction—or an argument on why they are wrong or why their experience is invalid, they will close up and be polarized against biblical truth. If I genuinely appreciate the Holy Spirit's work in the person's life and present to them the possibility they can receive a prophetic anointing to dramatically increase ministry power in their lives, they most often discover themselves quickly experiencing Spirit baptism with its biblical, confirming sign of tongues.

This focus on what are really secondary issues has also

produced a generation of ministers who suffer from what I call "acute pneumaphobia." That is, they are both convinced of the reality of Spirit baptism with evidential tongues, but at the same time, they are afraid it will ruin their church's dignified reputation. Is tongues speaking a necessary drudgery or a spiritually natural blessing? Is it like a vaccination, where you grit your teeth while the needle is going in before you can enjoy its long-term benefits? Do you "have to" speak in tongues or do you "get to"?

Speaking in tongues is not a liability, but a beautiful blessing. But power for ministry is the main feature of Spirit baptism. You don't have to be afraid of tongues ruining your church if you understand that the Baptism isn't just so people can speak in tongues but so they can speak to lost people with prophetic power.

If your approach to the Baptism is merely trying to convince the listener of a doctrine, the response will be limited. But if you teach that everyone can have a prophetic experience, trusting God to give them the right things to say to unbelievers, you'll be overwhelmed at the hungry response. I have discovered that how you approach people is critical—especially in a postmodern generation.

Misconception #3: *Where*

Have you ever listened to yourself tell someone how you were filled with the Holy Spirit? Preachers love to use Technicolor adjectives to describe their personal experiences. Perhaps you were in the spiritual "Area 51" when you were "beamed up" to the mother ship, seeing heavenly visions as you were being filled. Or maybe it wasn't actually that grand.

I bring this up not only to confront dishonesty—no matter how well-meaning a person may be—but to convey the dangerous assumptions the listener can draw from such descriptions of otherworldly close encounters.

The *where* I'm addressing refers not only to the atmosphere in which someone can receive the baptism in the

Holy Spirit, but also the actual venue. Is it only at red-hot camp meeting "Holy Ghost nights"? Or can someone receive after eating a stale doughnut at a men's prayer breakfast? Is it only after the minister has thoroughly rubbed his shoes on the wool carpet—and adequately static-charged his fingertips—or can it happen in someone's car on the way to work? I believe we have over-romanticized the reception process so much that many ordinary folks exclude themselves from receiving.

It's not nuclear physics; it's simple obedience. If you are firmly convinced that Jesus is the Baptizer in the Holy Spirit, then wherever He is, it can happen—and He's omnipresent.

One of the easiest traps to fall into is to place too much credence upon perceived emotional responses. Many ministers feel extreme, yet unnecessary, pressure to build emotionally charged atmospheres, places where their own personal testimony can be replicated for their congregations. I find it enlightening and burden-lightening to know that the Acts accounts of Spirit baptism never give one shred of emotional detail such as, "They were all filled and began to speak in other tongues as they cried precisely 1.4 ounces of tears." It is obvious that emotional responses are part of the way God made us, but it is also true they are secondary phenomena. Yet we still are more moved by what we can see rather than by the invisible reality. We have a tendency to misrepresent how the Baptism is received and then be disappointed when it doesn't happen our way.

When you minister on Spirit baptism, there are some exceptional days when you can almost hear the wind and see the fire of Acts 2. These are wonderful occurrences, but they are just that—exceptional. Many times I've witnessed large groups of people receive rather quietly; that's all right too. The point is they receive this new power to be God's prophetic mouthpieces.

Take your heavy backpack off! You don't have to create a highly charged atmosphere or be in a special meeting for people to be filled with the Holy Spirit. The bottom line is Jesus is the Baptizer, and He wants to show himself to people as their personal Baptizer in the Spirit today. Why not seize more opportunities—even nontraditional ones—to lead people into Spirit baptism?

Misconception #4: Who

This final reoccurring misconception has to do with the minister's self-concept. Many fall into the trap of believing they need a special gift to minister Spirit baptism—a gift they don't think they possess. Nothing could be further from the truth; only Jesus can baptize in the Holy Spirit.

It is true God gives unique spiritual passions to individuals and that special levels of faith can be cultivated for any area of ministry (evangelism, healing, compassion ministries, Spirit baptism, etc.). However, in ministering Spirit baptism—just as in witnessing—we merely present the truth and guide the way, but Jesus does the supernatural part. He always does the hard part. Like any spiritual process, you will become more at ease as you gain more experience.

The premise of our ministry is simply, "Jesus wants to." Jesus wants to save; Jesus wants to fill; Jesus wants to heal and restore. When you are firmly convinced that Jesus wants to fill people with His Spirit, you realize He will—as in every other area of ministry—supply what you lack to get the job done. He is the One with the special gift!

I mentioned that a special level of faith could be cultivated in this area. Let me explain. When I was first Spirit baptized at age twelve, I couldn't imagine why anyone else wouldn't want to receive it too. I began praying for all of my friends—and a few strangers—to receive the gift. In my zeal, God was gracious as some were filled; however, many were not. This was most likely due to my inexperience. Out of frustration I stumbled upon a prayer request that has since become a heartfelt fixture in my devotional life, "Father, give me the faith to believe that everyone I pray for will receive this gift." I'm not sure how it works exactly, but I've discovered that when you ask anything according to God's will, He hears you. Why not ask Him? Since you know that Jesus wants to baptize believers, why not partner with Him and give Him the opportunity to empower you with a greater level of faith? Why don't you pause and ask Him right now?

If you're still convinced there is a special gift necessary to minister Spirit baptism, why don't you ask God to give it to you?

Now that we've looked at some of the most common misconceptions, let's move on to the actual process of ministering Spirit baptism.

THE NUTS AND BOLTS OF MINISTERING SPIRIT BAPTISM

When I say "nuts and bolts," it could either be a euphemism for the practical side of the matter or a direct reference to the shenanigans that have been pulled over the years in full gospel circles— "a bunch of nuts waiting for a bolt from heaven" (or at least a vigorous slap on the head by an overly enthusiastic evangelist). You decide.

Nuts

When I was praying to receive the baptism in the Holy Spirit, it seemed that every evangelist who came through town would pray for me and wrestle me to the ground. It got to the place that whenever I'd see an evangelist, I wanted to just lie down on the floor and get it over with! So many seekers can testify that their personal altar workers were like Larry, Moe, and Curly—poking, slapping, and even sometimes breaking out the anvils and mallets. We have to laugh at ourselves sometimes.

Bolts

Is a bolt of lightning really coming from heaven? Or perhaps a jolt from a holy defibrillator? We have to sensitively frame a proper set of expectations for people before they receive and, at the same time, be understanding of their fears and apprehensions.

Manners and Mannerisms

Along these lines, I encourage you to build an easy-going, low-pressure atmosphere. Not that there is low expectancy, just low pressure. Seekers are often tense about receiving this gift; we don't want to add any more unnecessary anxiety. This can be done simply by having an understanding demeanor as you deal with them: "I know this is all new to you, but there is no reason to be afraid or stressed out. You want Jesus to fill you and Jesus wants to fill you, right? It's simple."

Think about your own spiritual life. Do you receive from God best when you feel tense or do you receive better when you are at ease? You probably do better when you're not put on the spot, because putting people at ease makes the whole process much easier—and more enjoyable, too. The goal is to be attuned to both the Spirit and the seeker simultaneously.

How about having a bunch of strangers ruffle your hair and wrinkle your clothes? Our present culture is extremely sensitive about personal space, so we need to be extra cautious about violating these invisible safety zones. This is why I almost always ask if I can gently place a hand on the seeker's shoulder before I pray; a shoulder is most often a nonthreatening place to touch. I haven't crushed a Mohawk or deflated a bouffant yet (though I did accidentally knock off a wig once!). We can be so distracting in our mannerisms and lack of manners that we become a roadblock for the person who wants to receive. Talk about being counterproductive!

As I mentioned earlier, I frequently ask if I can gently place a hand on the person's shoulder. Pushiness is not a fruit of the Spirit, but gentleness is. I have dealt with many seekers whose experience mirrors my own. They faced an overzealous minister trying to induce Spirit baptism by a chiropractic treatment. This is where sensitivity to the Spirit and to the person makes a significant difference. I will often ask a person who appears fearful to kneel with me. In this way, the fear of "free-falling" is greatly diminished and another distraction is eliminated. By the way, falling over doesn't function as biblical evidence of either Spirit baptism or as a signpost of any stage in the process of receiving.

So, first set an intentional atmosphere with a calm, understanding demeanor. Be careful of distracting mannerisms or of violating the seeker's personal space.

Anticipation and Expectations

Next, how do you tell a seeker what to anticipate without creating a false or exceptional set of expectations? The answer is in the Scriptures. The Book of Acts has a simple pattern that is repeated three times when people received Spirit baptism: Acts 2 (on Pentecost), Acts 10 (at Cornelius's house), and Acts 19 (in Ephesus) all record the same basic pattern.

The first step in the Acts pattern is to draw near to Jesus. The Acts recipients were focusing on Jesus as they were worshipping or listening to teaching about Him. Jesus was the focus because Jesus is the Baptizer. I like to use Luke 24 as a way of fleshing out how to focus on Jesus. Verse 53 shows us they were pressing in and worshipping Jesus continuously—that's a great place to start.

The second step in the biblical pattern is that the Holy Spirit will come upon the seeker. In Acts, at some stage in each of the processes, the Holy Spirit came upon everyone who received. You can trace the usage of the Greek verb *epi* ("to come upon") in conjunction with episodes of Spirit baptism in Acts. In every occurrence the Holy Spirit came upon everyone who received. You can confidently assure the seeker that the Holy Spirit will come upon them at some time while they are seeking. I always like to demystify this further, "You may or you may not be overcome with goose bumps, but you will at least be gently aware of His presence descending upon you at some distinct time."

The third step in the pattern involves the seeker yielding his voice to the Spirit's prompting. Simply stated, the believer gives his or her voice to God. The first step is initiated by the seeker as he chooses to draw near to Christ in worship. The second step is initiated by Christ as He sends the Holy Spirit upon the hungry seeker. The third step is a cooperative effort between the seeker and the Holy Spirit. The Spirit gives the ability to speak and the person does the actual speaking.

I have consistently witnessed the benefit of letting seekers know what to expect—so much "fear of the unknown" is then eliminated. Even the first Pentecostals had some idea of what to expect. As Christ had previously told them, *He* would "send

[them] what my Father has promised" them (Luke 24:49), that they would be "clothed with power" (Luke 24:49), and that they would "speak in new tongues" (Mark 16:17). Another benefit of setting biblical expectations is that the seeker can recognize his or her progress in the reception process.

The Real Nuts and Bolts

The first step in ministering on Spirit baptism is personal spiritual preparation. Have you prayed about the event? Do you have a word from God? Have you asked for His help and guidance? Have you asked for an increase of faith for ministering the Baptism?

The second step involves the teaching or preaching. Simplicity, not brilliance, is what helps people to receive. I have found the more simply I define what Spirit baptism is and what it is for, the more people want to receive it. Simplicity should also be the watchword for the explanation on how to receive. One of the easiest mistakes to make—and I have made this error many times—is to preach on the Baptism and never tell anyone how to receive it. It's information without function. It's like a person buying a new computer with no instructions. If you're not sure how to explain this, take some time and create your own bullet points, then go over them again to make sure they are easily understood.

So, let's assume there has been a simple teaching accurately defining the purpose of Spirit baptism followed by an equally simple explanation of how someone can receive it. The next step is to give opportunity for people to respond and receive. Many times I use the following procedure.

I like to make a dual application to the teaching, such as, "In a moment we will have some prayer time for those who want to receive this gift (specific application). But before we do that, how many would really like to experience a fresh touch from the Holy Spirit today (general application)?" This dual application engages almost everyone in the room. Though not all may feel ready to receive now and perhaps some have already received, almost all can affirm their desire for a fresh encounter with the Holy Spirit. When you feel the consensus in the room, invite everyone to step forward and pray for a few minutes. Inviting everyone to respond together also helps remove the first-time seeker's potential fear of being the "only needy one."

When people begin to gather and pray, I'll casually ask, "How many want to be baptized in the Holy Spirit for the first time?" When they respond, I'll typically ask them to listen as I restate the three steps to receive—draw near to Jesus, the Holy Spirit will come upon the seeker, and the seeker must yield his or her voice to God. This reinforces biblical expectations for the process.

This is where you, as the minister, can start feeling levels of anxiety and pressure to produce results. Don't go there. Only Jesus can baptize someone in the Holy Spirit, so relax! You have been obedient to proclaim this biblical truth, Now, your only job is to be sensitive to the Holy Spirit and to the people you are there to help. Jesus will do the hard part.

I like to lead a simple worship chorus to help people sensitize their hearts to God. *Hunger plus worship equals an amazingly easy atmosphere in which people can receive.* When the song is over, I encourage them to begin to praise Jesus out loud. In just a few moments, people will begin to receive.

After several minutes, I will ask, "How many have received so far and have the proof of a new spiritual language?" After they respond, I will then say, "If you haven't yet received, that's fine. Sometimes it takes a little while. However, there's never a wasted moment in seeking Christ. If you have a few more minutes, please continue to seek Him." I'll then begin to minister to people individually, taking time to listen to the Holy Spirit's leading. He will help you if you slow down and listen to His voice.

I also try to pay special attention to those who are very introverted. Many times "loners" struggle to receive in a group setting, so be sensitive to the way they are wired. I will frequently ask such a person, "Are you more quiet in your worship? That's fine. Some people receive better by themselves. Do you think you can find a quiet place where you can be alone in the next day or so?" I encourage them to do so as soon as possible and remind them of the three steps to receive. Many times they receive in their car on their way home from church! They are hungry, and Jesus wants to baptize them.

It is important to reinforce that sometimes it can take a little while because some personalities are very impatient and can easily become frustrated, or worse yet, discouraged.

Finally, I instruct those who have received to try out their new prophetic power as soon as possible. "Visit with a lost person and give God the opportunity to speak through you in the next day or so. You now have proof that you can say what God wants you to say." Otherwise, they can follow the path of many previous Pentecostals and think it is okay to have the power and to do nothing with it. We don't need any more "pew potatoes." People who have experienced the Holy Spirit's power yet refuse to be obedient to witness tend to get rather frustrated and infectiously grumpy.

CONCLUSION

I am absolutely convinced from the Scriptures and personal experience that God is still moving in Pentecostal power. I am equally convinced we must contend for a fresh demonstration of His power in our churches and our communities. We must cling to the biblical imperatives of Spirit baptism and its accompanying sign of tongues speaking; but we must also frame these truths in the practical, utilitarian ways the Bible presents.

If you don't think the models you've witnessed in the past would fly in your church context, don't throw the truth out with the bad model. Strategize with the Holy Spirit. Let Him anoint you with creativity to present and minister this truth in unique, non-traditional ways. After all, we can't do the job without the power.

CHAPTER TWO

CONFESSIONS OF A CHRONIC SEEKER

By Randy Hurst

In my Pentecostal upbringing, I really wanted the Holy Spirit baptism, but I didn't receive it for seven years. I was what some people referred to as a "chronic seeker." It wasn't until I reached a point of desperation for what only the Spirit could provide that I finally received.

There were a number of reasons why I believe it took me so long to receive. Much of the problem was *misunderstanding*. By understanding certain facts about the Holy Spirit baptism, I believe I would have received much sooner. Here are some things I wish I had understood.

THE PURPOSE OF THE HOLY SPIRIT BAPTISM

For the seven years I waited, I was wanting the Holy Spirit baptism for the wrong reason. I wanted it simply so I could say that I had it. For the most part, the purpose of this wonderful blessing escaped me. I wrongly viewed the Baptism as a point of arrival instead of what it is—a point of entrance into a life of Spirit-empowered witness for Christ.

Jesus clearly stated that the essential purpose of the Spirit's empowerment is to be His witnesses. The Holy Spirit baptism is a gift to all believers. But receiving the gift is not a guarantee that the promised power will be used for its intended purpose.

I heard an intriguing fact on the radio: 95 percent of all sport utility vehicles sold in the United States are never taken off-road. Of course, during Minnesota winters, four-wheel drive is a great help in snow and even on city streets. But why would someone need four-wheel drive on the freeways of Southern California? These vehicles were equipped for a purpose for which most are rarely, if ever, used.

This illustration can compare to many people's experience concerning the Holy Spirit baptism. They receive this wonderful gift, yet they don't put it into action or even fully understand the purpose for which this equipping power was given.

Jesus' promise to His followers was that they would be His witnesses wherever they went. Unfortunately, many equate being a witness merely with their speech, or what has come to be termed "witnessing." But effectiveness in reaching the spiritually lost requires a witness beyond words.

The apostle Paul wrote to the believers at Thessalonica: "Our gospel did not come to you in word only, but also in power and in the Holy Spirit and with full conviction; just as you know what kind of men we proved to be among you for your sake" (1 Thessalonians 1:5, NASB).

Paul's witness was not merely what he said ("not...in word only"), but also how he said it ("in power and in the Holy Spirit and with full conviction") and who he was ("you know what kind of men we proved to be among you for your sake").

The Holy Spirit empowers our witness in what we say. As He did for the New Testament Christians after the Day of Pentecost, the Spirit gives us the internal motivation to speak about Jesus, confident in His (the Spirit's) convincing work. The early Christians prayed for that kind of help: "Grant that Your bond-servants may speak Your word with all confidence" (Acts 4:29, NASB).

The Holy Spirit also helps us in how we speak. He moves us in our witness with a sincere, compelling passion.

And the Holy Spirit enables our character to become

what God has called us to be as the fruit of the Spirit—the nature of Jesus Christ—becomes evident in our lives.

JESUS IS THE BAPTIZER

Just before Jesus ascended to heaven, He told His disciples,

> Thus it is written, that the Christ would suffer and rise again from the dead the third day, and that repentance for forgiveness of sins would be proclaimed in His name to all the nations, beginning from Jerusalem. You are witnesses of these things. And behold, *I am sending forth the promise* of My Father upon you; but you are to stay in the city until you are clothed with power from on high (Luke 24:46–49, NASB, emphasis added).

On the Day of Pentecost, Peter preached, "God has raised this Jesus to life, and we are all witnesses of the fact. Exalted to the right hand of God, *he has received* from the Father the promised Holy Spirit *and has poured out* what you now see and hear" (Acts 2:32,33, NASB, emphasis added). Notice that *Jesus* is the Baptizer!

Part of my problem for years was that I was seeking an experience rather than the Person who gives that experience. When people seek for the Baptism, they should shut the door on outside distractions and center their minds and hearts on Jesus. He is the Baptizer, and He will fill them.

THE NATURE OF THE SPIRIT'S EMPOWERMENT

People often think of the Holy Spirit's empowerment only in terms of signs and wonders and spiritual gifts. But the word translated "power" in Acts 1:8 is wonderfully comprehensive. It simply means "ability" and applies in practical ways to everyday life.

The Holy Spirit supplies whatever it takes to help us accomplish what is needed. That is all we really need—whatever it takes.

The Holy Spirit enables ordinary people to do extraordinary things.

The power Jesus promised His followers is for every aspect of Christian living, enabling us to do and be whatever our Lord has purposed in our lives.

THE HOLY SPIRIT BAPTISM IS A GIFT

The promise of the Holy Spirit is for every believer. The apostle Peter said, "The promise is for you and your children and for all who are far off—for all whom the Lord our God will call" (Acts 2:39, NASB).

I believe many seekers of the Holy Spirit baptism struggle with the same issue I did—the belief or feeling that we have to be "good enough" to receive the gift. Simply put, the Holy Spirit baptism cannot be earned; it is a gift. Every believer who has been saved by grace is qualified to receive this wonderful promise.

During the time of my youth, a teaching or idea circulated among Pentecostal churches that I believe was misleading and wrong. It stated that the Holy Spirit would only dwell in a "clean vessel." We believed we had to cleanse ourselves to make us ready to receive the gift. In reality, the blood of Christ has already cleansed us from sin. Personal battles of the flesh cannot be won by our own efforts to prepare ourselves to receive the Holy Spirit. The Holy Spirit will cleanse and transform us. When we understand that, we can seek the Spirit and receive the wonderful gift of the Baptism by faith alone, not by any works that we can do.

Even so, many who know this truth intellectually are hesitant to seek. Some feel they don't deserve this blessing. But the Holy Spirit baptism is promised to every believer. The apostle Paul taught that we receive the promise of the Spirit by faith (Galatians 3:14).

If someone has received Jesus Christ as Savior, he or she is already qualified to receive the Holy Spirit baptism. Seekers of the Baptism need to understand that they don't have to become better than they are to deserve the gift the Lord has promised them.

Paul compares our spiritual lives to clay jars. He says, "We have this treasure in jars of clay to show that this all-surpassing power is from God and not from us" (2 Corinthians 4:7). Clay has imperfections. So do we. God knows that. He receives us as we are and will fill us with the Holy Spirit, who will enable us to change.

We must recognize our need of His power. Many believers speak of needing more of God. The issue for most of us is really that God needs more of us. Make room for His fullness by surrendering every area of your life to Jesus' lordship and invite Him to fill you with the Spirit to empower you to live for Him.

THE GIFT IS RECEIVED BY FAITH

Jesus' disciples had to wait for God to "pour out of His Spirit" as He promised through the prophet Joel. When someone seeks Spirit baptism today, they do not have to wait in the same way the disciples did. The Spirit's outpouring took place on the Day of Pentecost once and for all. Now we seek His inpouring individually.

When we seek, we need not worry about having a false experience or that when we speak in tongues it will be from our imagination. Jesus taught:

> Ask, and it will be given to you; seek, and you will find; knock, and it will be opened to you. For everyone who asks, receives; and he who seeks, finds; and to him who knocks, it will be opened. Now suppose one of you fathers is asked by his son for a fish; he will not give him a snake instead of a fish, will he? Or if he is asked for an egg, he will not give him a scorpion, will he? If you then, being evil, know how to give good gifts to your children, how much more will your heavenly Father give the Holy Spirit to those who ask Him? (Matthew 7:7–11, NASB).

The tense used in the original language of the New Testament implies a continuous action. It means, "Keep asking, keep seeking, keep knocking, and you will receive." The fullness of the Holy Spirit is a promise to every believer and is received by faith.

If people sincerely seek the Lord for what He has promised, God will give them what they ask for. Some seekers find it helpful to have other Spirit-filled believers pray with them. Others are more comfortable seeking alone.

WHO DOES THE SPEAKING

One of my greatest struggles was that I was, to a significant extent, passive in my seeking—especially concerning the aspect of speaking in tongues. I spent hours at the altar, "seeking" to be filled. And even though I believe my motive was good, I was "waiting on the Lord" to speak through me.

Scripture is very clear. The Holy Spirit *enables* us to speak in tongues. He does not take control of us like a puppet. We do the speaking. The Holy Spirit enables us to speak.

We don't know why God chose speaking in tongues as a sign of the Spirit's empowerment. Some believe the reason is found in the teaching of James, who says that "no one can tame the tongue" (James 3:8, NASB). But that idea can actually be misleading to people because they might expect the Holy Spirit to take control of their tongue. Acts 2:4 states that: "All of them were filled with the Holy Spirit and began to speak in other tongues as the Spirit enabled them." The Spirit "enabled"—He did not control. Although the Holy Spirit enables us, we do the speaking.

THE PURPOSES OF PRAYING IN THE SPIRIT

Three dramatic signs accompanied the outpouring of the Holy Spirit on the Day of Pentecost: a sound like a rushing mighty wind, tongues of fire appearing on the believers' heads, and speaking with other tongues (languages). The wind and fire were not repeated in Acts, but speaking with tongues continued to occur when people were filled with the Spirit.

To fully understand the significance of the outpouring of the Holy Spirit on the Day of Pentecost, we must remember that the Book of Acts is a sequel to the Gospel of Luke. Luke and Acts are actually a two-volume work concerning the lives of Jesus and His followers. To understand the first part of Acts, we must go back to the last part of Luke and remember Jesus' final instructions and commands to His followers. Read Luke 24:46–49 again.

Jesus' command was that a message of "repentance for forgiveness of sins would be proclaimed in His name to all the nations" (verse 47). It is difficult to imagine a more convincing sign to assure the disciples that they had truly been "clothed with power from on high" than speaking in languages they had never learned.

A few sincere Christians have interpreted this to mean that missionaries who are filled with the Holy Spirit do not have to learn other languages. I know two missionaries who temporarily received the miracle of being able to speak in the language of the area where they were ministering. However, it happened only once in their lives under very unusual circumstances and was never repeated. Such miracles could be termed "extraordinary," much as Luke described the healings in Acts 19 when handkerchiefs and aprons touched by Paul were taken to the sick. We don't totally understand why God uses the manifestation of speaking in tongues, but it certainly is a sign that God is doing something supernatural.

Scripture records that praying in tongues has several purposes in the lives of Spirit-filled believers.

Confirmation

Speaking in tongues is the first outward sign of the Holy Spirit baptism. This is found in Acts 2:4 and also in Acts 10 and 19. Acts 10 is especially instructive, because Luke records that the Jewish believers were convinced that the Gentiles had received the gift of the Holy Spirit when they heard them "speaking with tongues and exalting God" (verse 46, NASB). In rare circumstances, the Spirit will enable a person to speak in a language that is unknown to the speaker but known to someone who is present. This can also be a confirmation to others—especially nonbelievers.

I grew up in East Africa where my parents were missionaries. I remember well an incredible testimony concerning someone speaking with other tongues. An African man and his wife came forward in a church service to receive Christ. When the pastor prayed for them, the woman was filled with the Holy Spirit. She began to worship and praise God eloquently in English. After her time of worship and prayer the pastor, who was fluent in English, spoke to her in English and she didn't understand a word.

Many years ago, my uncle Bud Abbott was leading the regular Wednesday night Bible study and prayer meeting at the Assembly of God in Superior, Wisconsin. During the prayer time, a godly deacon who worked for the railroad began praying quietly in tongues. The group fell silent and listened as he prayed in the Spirit for about ten minutes.

When he finished praying, a visiting woman stood and gave this testimony. Passing through town, she had seen a light in the church and slipped in the back. A missionary to Tibet for twenty years, she told the congregation that the deacon had been praying in the Tibetan dialect she knew. He was praying for a Christian in China by name who was suffering under tremendous persecution.

Adoration

Our finite minds are incapable of comprehending and our own language is inadequate to totally express our worship to God. Speaking in tongues, in what many refer to as a "prayer language," frees us to communicate the worship of our hearts that is inexpressible in our limited vocabulary. Having been a missionary, I can converse in more than one language, but I still run out of words in worship to God. When I pray in tongues, the Holy Spirit bears witness with my spirit that the worship of my heart is being communicated with His help.

Edification

Praying in the Spirit edifies—builds up—in two ways: It edifies the individual who prays in the Spirit, and if interpreted, it edifies the church. Paul stated that he spoke in tongues more than all of the Corinthians, yet he reminded them that in the church setting tongues should be interpreted so that all could be edified (1 Corinthians 14:5). This does not restrict the private use of tongues for personal edification, because praying in tongues builds up the believer spiritually.

With the stresses, pressures, and challenges of life, we have the blessing of praying in the Spirit beyond our own wisdom and understanding. The best way to begin every day is with prayer. The gift of praying in tongues enables us to pray beyond ourselves for each day, not knowing what we will face. The Holy Spirit prays through us to effectively seek God's divine help in everyday living.

Intercession

"The Spirit also helps our weakness; for we do not know how to pray as we should" (Romans 8:26, NASB). When we pray in the Spirit, He enables us to pray beyond our understanding. Paul said, "With all prayer and petition pray at all times in the Spirit, and with this in view, be on the alert with all perseverance and petition for all the saints" (Ephesians 6:18, NASB). God uses us to work His purposes in the lives of others through the ministry of intercession.

Petition

The Spirit prays *through* us and *for* us. We are told by the apostle Paul that we don't know how to pray as we ought. We don't know what to really ask for, and we often "ask amiss" because our motives are wrong. The Spirit both prays beyond and transforms our motives. Consequently, in His empowerment, we can petition the Father and Son for things the Spirit *knows* we need, instead of what we *think* we need.

Praying in the Spirit is a wonderful part of the Holy Spirit's empowerment. It confirms the experience of the Holy Spirit baptism, empowers us to effective worship, builds us up spiritually, and enables us both to intercede for others and petition God for our own needs beyond our own intelligence and wisdom.

Speaking in tongues continued to occur throughout the Book of Acts when people were filled with the Spirit. The same is true today. This experience is for everyone who receives the Holy Spirit baptism.

PERSEVERANCE

I really like the wording in the Assemblies of God statement of foundational truths regarding the baptism in the Holy Spirit. It reads, "All believers are entitled to and should *ardently expect and earnestly seek* the promise of the Father, the baptism in the Holy Spirit and fire, according to the command of our Lord Jesus Christ" (emphasis mine). When it states that believers should "ardently expect and earnestly seek," it speaks not only of seeking with expectation but doing so *ardently* and *earnestly*. We should seek fervently but not fearfully. Persevere in faith to receive what our Lord has promised.

If a person does not receive the Baptism immediately, he or she should continue to seek the Lord Jesus in faith. God's promise and desire is to baptize each believer with the Holy Spirit.

KEEP BEING FILLED

Seeking the Holy Spirit baptism is not a one-time event, but rather a commitment to continue seeking the Spirit's fullness for the rest of one's life. The Old Testament account of the Israelites' exodus from Egypt records that God gave them bread from heaven, called manna, to feed them during their wilderness journey. It was not a supply to be stored up and carried with them. It was given to them as they needed it.

A life overflowing with the fullness of the Spirit is much the same. When Paul exhorted the Ephesians Christians to be filled with the Spirit, the tense of the verb means to "keep on being filled." The infilling of the Spirit should be ongoing. We must keep praying in the Spirit, loving in the Spirit, and living in the Spirit. The Holy Spirit baptism—as wonderful as it is—is not a one-time experience. We need a continual inpouring of the Spirit daily in our lives, as the apostle Paul says in Ephesians 5:18.

CONCLUSION

A familiar saying is "Hindsight is 20/20." In other words, when we look back on past experiences, we see circumstances more clearly. We learn through life's lessons and are able to pass on wisdom to others. Hopefully, you will use the insights and Scriptures given in this chapter to help others receive the gift of the Holy Spirit without being hindered by the misunderstandings that kept me from receiving for seven years.

CHAPTER THREE

Preparing Yourself to Help Others

By Ken Cramer

I served for five years under a senior pastor who had a powerful gift of praying for people to receive the baptism in the Holy Spirit. Though he was a great teacher, he didn't teach them at the altar. He inspired them to seek the Spirit at the altar and followed up with the laying on of hands. Many people were filled with the Spirit through his ministry.

My attempts to follow in his footsteps failed miserably. This disconnect was due mainly to my inability to inspire people to come to the altar. I would lay hands on seekers but seldom had success. I began reading everything I could about the Baptism in the Spirit. I then decided to watch the crowd and target people. I'd look to see if there was passion expressed in worship or whether they were really pressing in to seek God. If they weren't, I would ask them, "Has anyone ever talked to you about being filled with the Spirit?" Then I would take the person through the accounts in the Book of Acts of people receiving the Spirit, and the Word builds faith in them to receive.

I share this story because it taught me there are at least three ways taught in Scripture for people to receive the Baptism. The first is at an outpouring, when everyone around receives. God moves through the preaching of the Word, people are seeking, no one is laying hands on anyone, and people get filled (Acts 2; 10). Second, people in Scripture received the Baptism through the laying on of hands (Acts 8; 9; 19). Third, and also implicit in the foregoing passages, is through teaching and instruction. This involves sharing the Word, personal testimony, faith building, and removal of unsound doctrine so that the person receives.

I challenge the people I pastor to find which method works for them in leading others into the Baptism. In our congregation, we have a few young adults who just get around people seeking the Baptism and worship with them for a few minutes and the seekers are filled every time. In fact, these young people tell seekers, "We won't lay hands on you because we want you to be totally convinced God did it." These radical worshippers set an atmosphere and environment that is charged with the anointing, and people just get baptized in the Spirit.

Others in our church are more analytical. They explain the Scriptures, lay a teaching foundation, and steadily bring others into the experience. I believe the important thing is to explain to the congregation that a "one-size-fits-all" ministry mentality doesn't work. David didn't use Saul's armor while giant slaying. Likewise, if we'll teach our people a ministry-centered mindset, we might help them discover there are ways of doing ministry that work for them but would never work for us. We have to be okay with that fact.

Most importantly, I need to model to people the ministry of the baptism in the Holy Spirit. I was teaching a new members class recently with eleven students. Most were already filled with the Spirit and used supernatural language regularly. After I taught on the subject of being filled with the Spirit, one person said, "Well, you've answered all of the questions I had, but how do I get this?"

I only hesitated for a second before I pointed to Luke 11 and said, "It's written here that if you ask your earthly father for something, he will gladly give it to you. Jesus said your Heavenly Father wants even more to give the Holy Spirit to those who ask."

Then I looked at the young man and said, "Are you ready to ask and receive?"

His response was, "Of course." He asked. And he received. It was that simple. No wind, no fire, but tongues and power, just as we should expect.

The class erupted in worship! We watched the supernatural happen right there in a new members class! Several of those new members have since led others to Spirit fullness because they now understand the simplicity of receiving and appreciate the necessity of being filled with God's Spirit.

Here are some of the keys I employ when sharing how to minister the baptism in the Holy Spirit. I encourage people who want to be used in this way to examine their own lifestyle and let God build them up as a person. Remember, one of the uses of the baptism in the Spirit is for personal edification. Let me share these keys with you.

LIVE A SPIRITUALLY DISCIPLINED LIFE

When you are speaking to someone about his or her relationship with the Holy Spirit, you first need to consider your own relationship with the Holy Spirit. I like to follow Christ's example through Luke 4 as He was "led by the Spirit" into the wilderness and fasted forty days. Jesus' fasting was under the leadership of the Spirit of God. He was not fasting as a special sacrifice, nor was He fasting in order to find God's will. Jesus lived the will of God. We as believers are in the will of God as we walk with Him daily.

No, Jesus fasted so His flesh would not be a hindrance when He confronted the enemy. I believe every time you begin to lead someone into Spirit baptism you will confront things that attempt to distract and derail that person from receiving this infinitely powerful gift of the Holy Spirit—misunderstandings, fears, ignorance of the Scriptures, maybe even demonic forces. Understand that when someone is saved, it is personal for them. But when they are filled with the Spirit, the public message of the resurrected Jesus will show up and really make the devil mad! In Acts 2:33 Peter said, "This same Jesus has poured out what you see and hear." The baptism in the Holy Spirit is a menace to the enemy's methods of enslaving and entrapping because the anointing breaks every yoke of bondage.

Jesus fasted so His sensitivity to the work of the Spirit

would be heightened and in control. Jesus said that the student is not above his master, so occasional fasting will keep your flesh in check and your spirit tuned in to what God wants to happen when you are leading others into the Baptism.

LET SCRIPTURE FILL IN THE BLANKS IN YOUR UNDERSTANDING

It is important that you spend time understanding what the Scriptures have to say about the baptism in the Holy Spirit. Be clear and confident about what to expect so you can communicate it to others. A basic rule of thumb for a clear understanding of Scripture goes like this:

1. What did God say and do in the Old Testament?
2. What did God say and do through the ministry of Jesus?
3. What did the Early Church in the New Testament consider normal?

When it comes to the ministry of the Spirit in the Old Testament, there are several helpful passages. Numbers 11:25–29 describes the Spirit coming upon the seventy appointed elders in Israel. Instead of Moses guarding his position as leader, he said, "Would God that all the LORD's people were prophets, and that the LORD would put his spirit upon them" (Numbers 11:29, KJV).

Through the prophet Joel, God said, "I will pour out my spirit upon all flesh" (Joel 2:28, KJV). This gives you a hint of God's desire to be among His people.

My favorite area in Scripture to study the Baptism is the Book of Acts. Acts 2, 8, 9, 10, and 19 all contain vital information regarding the outpouring of the Holy Spirit and the Spirit's work in the Early Church.

In Acts 2, three supernatural signs accompanied the Spirit's outpouring: sound of wind, flames of fire, and supernatural language or speaking in tongues.

In Acts 8, Peter and John began laying hands on people to receive the Holy Spirit. Though no outward signs are listed in the passage, Simon, a local sorcerer, tried to buy the gift they were handing out. He saw a business venture in the making. What did Simon see? Obviously, some kind of reaction among the people he interpreted as a commodity for resale in the public market!

In Acts 9, Ananias laid hands on Saul who was healed and filled with the Spirit. By Paul's own words in 1 Corinthians 14:18, supernatural language was a profound part of his life.

Peter's vision in Acts 10 prepared him to witness to the Gentiles and invite them into a thoroughly Jewish church. Peter went to the house of a man named Cornelius who had had his own encounter with angels. Peter took some Jewish believers with him to the house of an "unclean" Gentile. As Peter preached, God took the altar call out of his hands and the Gentiles began to speak in tongues and praise God. Peter was dumfounded. As his legalism melted away, Peter asked, "Can anyone keep these people from being baptized with water? They have received the Holy Spirit *just as we have*" (Acts 10:47, emphasis added).

What physical sign did the Jewish believers see that caused Peter to use the words "just as we have"? Was there a sound of wind? No. Were there flames? No. Just people yielding themselves and receiving their own supernatural language as the Holy Spirit came upon them (verse 46). It was this physical evidence that caused Peter and the other Jews to call for water baptism and acceptance of the Gentiles into the church!

In Acts 19, Paul stressed once again the need for the Spirit when he asked a group of believers, "Did you receive the Holy Spirit when you believed?" (verse 1). So many things could have been asked, but Paul stressed the urgency of being filled with the Spirit. After building up the disciples' faith, he laid hands on them and they were filled, spoke in tongues, and prophesied.

Remember, as you meditate on the Scriptures regarding the outpouring of the Holy Spirit, God will give you greater insight and build up your faith on the subject. If you will meditate on the Scriptures, the Holy Spirit will give you great confidence in what He can offer to others through you. You come with good news! Jesus wants to use you in the power of the Holy Spirit to further His kingdom. There is a desperate need for people to receive the Holy Spirit's fullness. Since Jesus is the One who actually does the baptizing, shouldn't we be willing and available to assist Him by helping people prepare to receive?

ASK GOD TO REVEAL SPIRITUAL ROADBLOCKS

Your task is like that of John the Baptist—you are there to prepare the way of the Lord. Take out the rough places and flatten the terrain so that the way is clear for people to receive the Holy Spirit. Jesus knew what was in a man. We have to know what is happening in a person before we can adequately minister to them. Obviously, you can't know all their thoughts, but you can ask questions and discover where they are on the subject of the Holy Spirit.

Assuming you have already led them to Christ in prayer or have knowledge of their profession of faith, you are ready to proceed. Sometimes asking what they have heard before about receiving the Baptism is helpful. You might need to correct some wrong thinking. For example, if they fail to realize that the Spirit is here to be received (an active term) and not just to be waited for (a passive term), they won't be seeking effectively. Tell them that the promise of the Holy Spirit has been fulfilled since Pentecost and the Spirit is ready for them to receive. What are they waiting for?

Listen carefully when you ask questions like "What have you been taught about the Holy Spirit?" or "Have you ever asked God to make himself real to you?" You might share an example from Acts to build their faith in what God wants to do for them.

Think of this ministry in terms of aligning the seeker's spirit, soul, and body. I'll explain. If they are born-again, their spirit wants more of God. They are already hungry. If they have had wrong teaching, their mind has been subjected to a wrong understanding about the Holy Spirit and needs to line up with the hunger of their spirit. If they are totally ignorant about the Holy

Spirit, you need to educate them. Once the mind is ready to receive, tell them what to expect from God.

Tell them practical things without being overly emotional. Prepare them to receive by saying, "You might hear words in your spirit" or "You might feel a tension on your tongue." Encourage them to yield to God in praise and to open their mouth and release the language He wants to flow through them. This lines them up completely with what the Holy Spirit wants to do in their spirit, soul, and body.

Give seekers as much understanding as you can, but bring them to the place where they have to reach out in faith. Periodically ask, "Are you ready to receive?" This helps them be ready to step out. It might be sooner than you think.

Having shown them the five instances in Acts where the Holy Spirit was poured out, including the three times when the believers spoke in supernatural language, ask them, "Are you ready to receive the Holy Spirit just as they have?" If they answer "No" or "I'm not sure" or "I'm not ready," ask them what they need you to be clearer about. Don't pray for them or lay hands on them yet. Wait until they can say out loud, "Yes, I see it in the Word," or "I believe that I'll receive when you lay hands on me like Paul did in Acts 19." If you don't get their verbal affirmation and you attempt to override their apprehension with your passion, you'll both be disappointed.

But when they say, "Yes, I'll receive," their commitment is evident. They will be praying in a supernatural language, usually very quickly.

Preparing yourself is important when helping others receive the Baptism. Sensitivity to the Holy Spirit and dependence on God's Word will give you wisdom and faith as you talk and pray with seekers. Jesus baptizes people in different settings and in different ways, and wonderful experiences come as a result of being prepared and following the Lord's leading as He helps you help others.

CHAPTER FOUR

MINISTERING THE HOLY SPIRIT BAPTISM IN TODAY'S CULTURE

By Gary Grogan

Many pastors in Spirit-filled movements speak in tongues as a part of their daily devotional habit but don't preach or teach on the Holy Spirit baptism, especially on a Sunday morning. They fear the risk of turning someone off or causing confusion in their church fellowships. While they believe the baptism in the Holy Spirit is a viable biblical experience and have personally experienced the language of the Spirit, they rarely, if ever, teach what the Bible says about the baptism in the Holy Spirit. Certainly there have been abuses and misuses in manifestations of the Holy Spirit, and this is a valid concern among pastors and church leaders. In fact, some Spirit-filled churches become hyper-emotional, reaching very few if any, unchurched in their communities and simply turning off many people who are sincerely checking out the Christian faith.

Effective pastors and churches don't want to turn people off; they want to help people come to faith, and they work very hard to build bridges with the unchurched in their personal lives and communities. They have dedicated themselves to giving their very best efforts to see people become fully devoted followers of Jesus Christ. They are absolutely committed to the Great Commission through relevant evangelism and realistic discipleship. So how does ministering the Holy Spirit baptism in today's culture work?

Young pastors and church leaders I dialogue with are not struggling so much with the theology of the Holy Spirit baptism as they are with the methodology. How do we make this work in today's culture? How do we reach people and transfer our convictions about the Holy Spirit baptism without pushing them out the backdoor? These are honest questions with which we must cope.

I was visiting with Dr. Gordon Anderson, president of North Central University in Minneapolis, and he told me about a meeting he had with a middle-aged pastor who is also struggling with methodology. His church has grown; he is reaching unchurched people and seeing people come to faith in Christ. He told Dr. Anderson he thoroughly embraces the theology of the Holy Spirit baptism but cannot embrace tactics previously used. He said if he had an old-time, foot stomping, highly charged, emotional atmosphere his people would "freeze up, lock up, and walk out" simply because they would not be able to process the method—not the message—being presented.

The starting point for this pastor was that he believed the Holy Spirit baptism is truly biblical and viable for today. I have had this conversation many times with pastors of all ages and youth pastors who are reaching people but struggling with how to present the Holy Spirit in a way that will make their people want this experience and not walk out the backdoor. Let me say again loud and clear: If you want to minister the Holy Spirit baptism in today's culture, you must settle in your heart of hearts it is a true and needed experience. That is the starting point.

You must also be intentional in your approach. Because today's culture is so different from earlier cultures in our history, we must work harder at being creative in the way we present the Holy Spirit baptism. We teach on the Holy Spirit baptism right away in our first-level membership class, knowing we are preparing believers to eventually receive. We don't push, yet we regularly have people testify that they have received the Baptism. When I ask people in our congregation who have received the Holy Spirit baptism what motivated them to begin seeking, many times they have said something like, "Pastor, I heard you mention how much it helped you in your personal walk with God, and I just decided I needed this too." Intentionality is a great key to ministering the Holy Spirit baptism in today's culture.

PRACTICALLY LEADING OTHERS INTO THE HOLY SPIRIT BAPTISM

My wife, Bonnie, was not raised in a Pentecostal church. When an Assemblies of God church in her neighborhood started a bus ministry, her parents agreed to let their six girls attend. What a sacrifice for my father-in-law to get his six daughters out of the house every Sunday morning! Bonnie says she did not always understand the outward expressions of the worship in the services, but she was drawn in her heart and knew it was genuine. She would say to her sisters at times, "Did you feel what I felt in church today?"

One of our previous assistant pastors, Scott Hale, was raised in a traditional church and tells the story of being confirmed and anointed with oil. The pastor put his hand on Scott and said, "Receive the Holy Spirit." Scott says, "You know what happened? Nothing!" When he started attending our church, there were things about our worship he did not understand, and he would talk to his friends afterward about what he sensed in the services.

Bonnie and Pastor Scott were eventually baptized in the Holy Spirit and experienced the joy of praying in a language they had never learned. Even though some say this wonderful experience is no longer for today, I say if it is in the Bible, let's believe it, receive it, and experience it! Very likely if you are reading this, you already believe it is for today. However, we need more understanding on how to receive and experience the Holy Spirit baptism.

RECEIVING THE BAPTISM IN THE HOLY SPIRIT

Certainly you have to be active. You can't be passive and expect to receive. People say things like, "If God wants me to receive this experience, then He will just have to zap me or something." That is like saying, "If God wants to save me He will just have to zap me or something." It doesn't work that way. Of course He does the saving and the baptizing, but we have to call on the name of the Lord to be saved. It is the same way with the Holy Spirit baptism. Jesus put it this way in the Beatitudes, "Blessed are those who hunger and thirst for righteousness for they shall be filled" (Matthew 5:6). In other words, we have to be active; we have to be spiritually hungry.

When it comes to the Holy Spirit baptism, we take a step of faith by praying out loud. Because God has chosen speaking in languages never learned as the initial physical evidence of the Holy Spirit baptism, we have to be willing to pray out loud. If someone is unwilling to pray out loud, he or she will not be baptized in the Holy Spirit and enjoy praying in another language. To take a step of faith and be active in receiving, we have to pray out loud.

I am convinced one of the reasons the apostle Paul said he prayed in tongues more than everyone else is because of the beauty of it! (See 1 Corinthians 14:18.) Because it is so beautiful, no one needs to fear speaking in tongues, regardless of how different it may sound or how unusual it may seem. Many people who begin to speak in tongues stop because they think they are making up the words or it sounds strange to them. I always assure those seeking the Holy Spirit baptism that it may sound strange and that is okay, because some languages do sound strange to us. Then I refer them to Luke 11:11–13 and assure them God will not play tricks on them, so they are not making up the words. I tell them they are speaking in tongues because they are! It is their tongue, their vocal cords, their lips, and so on, and that is exactly what the Bible says. First Corinthians 14:2 and 4 mention someone speaking in a tongue. Acts 2:4 teaches that we do the speaking but the Holy Spirit gives us the utterance or the ability to speak. When these things are explained, people seem to receive more easily.

Second, in order to receive, you have to believe God wants you to have this wonderful experience (Galatians 3:14). Salvation, the Holy Spirit baptism, or any good thing—everything we receive from God we receive by faith. You have to believe!

Just as the enemy tries to convince us our salvation experience is not real, so he does with any experience we have with God, including this wonderful and enriching Holy Spirit baptism. It is true that what you are speaking may sound foolish to your intellect, but you have to believe.

Paul instructed believers to be filled with the Holy Spirit (Ephesians 5:18). So, if you are hungry, here is what you should do:

1. *Ask—look to Jesus!* He is the One who baptizes in the Holy Spirit (Matthew 3:11; Mark 1:8; Luke 3:16; John 1:33). He will not play tricks on us (Luke 11:11–13). Don't look to any man or group of people. Just ask Him: *Jesus, I ask You to baptize me in the Holy Spirit.*

2. *Praise.* Psalm 22:3 declares that God inhabits the praises of His people. The more you praise Him, the more His presence will increase in you. Eventually you won't know what to say in your own language, and, if you believe, you will speak in a language you have never learned. Say to Him: *Jesus, I believe that I will receive right now.*

3. *Now just speak in tongues.* God will give utterance. You do your part, which is to speak out, and God will do His part, which is to give you the ability to speak in a language you have never learned. It really is miraculous! In worship the Psalmist was praising God for Israel's deliverance, but I have used Psalm 81:10 for years to encourage people to take a step of faith when it comes to receiving the Holy Spirit baptism. It says, "Open wide your mouth and I will fill it" (NIV). It doesn't have to be in a dramatic, emotional way. I have seen literally thousands of people of all ages who, when they took that humble step of faith and opened their mouths, began speaking as the Spirit gave them utterance, a language they had never learned. It is always a joyous experience and, if not immediate, then it becomes joyful eventually!

Some articles I have read make it sound like the real days of Pentecost are behind us. I listened to a CD of popular pastor who hosted a world-renowned revival in his church say, "From my perspective, Pentecost in most of our churches is a thing of the past. We have lost it." I totally and completely disagree with him. Pentecost is not a style that comes from a certain part of the country. Pentecost is God's presence working among us, changing us, and using us to help people find their way to God. It is possible to minister the Holy Spirit baptism in a post-Christian culture. My prayer is that God will give you grace, and I know He will.

The calling of Jesus was clear: "to seek and to save what was lost" (Luke 19:10). That should be our purpose and calling as well. If we receive the Holy Spirit baptism with its initial evidence and we don't use the ability we have been given to reach out to unsaved people, we are spiritually dysfunctional and ineffective. I like the way evangelist Tim Enloe refers to tongues as the "first sign or first proof" of the Holy Spirit baptism and effective ministry and outreach as the "confirming sign or full proof" of being Spirit-filled. It is a two-part process, he says, of receiving and then giving it away.

Our Lord put it this way: "You will receive power when the Holy Spirit comes on you; and you will be my witnesses" (Acts 1:8). God help us to truly receive and then give away in compassionate ministry to the unbelievers around us. That is being Spirit-filled!

CHAPTER FIVE

PARTNERING WITH SEEKERS

By Judi Bullock

One Sunday night, a lady visited Calvary Temple in Seattle where my husband and I were pastoring. When my husband gave the altar call, she ran down to the altar weeping before God. I went to talk with her. She said she needed to accept Christ as her Savior, so I prayed with her. She was gloriously saved. Suddenly she covered her mouth. It appeared as if she was sticking her fingers in her mouth.

"Why are you covering your mouth?" I asked.

"These funny words are coming out," she said, "and I don't know what they are. I've never said them before."

I assured her, "That is the Holy Spirit."

She had never heard about the Holy Spirit. After I gave a quick explanation, she broke out in the most beautiful heavenly language. She wept, cried out to God, praised, and shouted. It was a glorious experience for her, me, and everyone present.

When she was done praying, she gave her testimony. "I was on drugs and my son is on drugs," she said. "I was cooking dinner for him tonight, and God said, 'Put your frying pan away. You go to church.' I heard Him as I've never heard anything. He clearly spoke to me, 'Go to church.'"

She obeyed, came to our church that night, and was saved and filled with the Holy Spirit all in one service. God knew exactly what she needed!

When I was growing up, my father was an evangelist. My mom and I traveled with him as much as we could. In his revival meetings, I used to watch my mother easily pray with people to receive the Holy Spirit. When I was nine, I said to my friend, "I'm going down there and I'm going to be filled with the Holy Spirit tonight; I'm not giving up until I get it." And that's exactly what happened! With hunger and a childlike faith, I received the Spirit shortly after I went down to pray.

In my teen years, I developed a hunger to pray with people to receive the Holy Spirit. My mother's passion was stirring in me. Years later, when my husband was district superintendent, I did a workshop and taught pastors' wives how to pray with people to receive the Holy Spirit. I was amazed so many of them did not know how to pray with people for this gift.

I remember one pastor making an appointment with my husband because he wanted me to pray with a young man who was going into the ministry, that he would receive the baptism in the Holy Spirit. It wasn't hard. The man knelt down by the platform with his face to the ground, and he quietly received the Holy Spirit.

Pastors have said to me, "I need you to come and pray with some people to be filled with the Spirit." *What's going on here?* I thought. *Why don't these pastors do it?* And then my husband said to me, "Honey, you love to pray people through." I never felt what I was doing was anything special. I have no degree behind my name; I just love to pray with people.

Then I realized something: If we do not start teaching this to our churches and our children, we're just one generation away from not having our people filled with the Holy Spirit. I was on a mission to get pastors to talk more about the Baptism and to give time in their churches for people to be filled with the Holy Spirit.

OPPORTUNITIES

When people receive Christ, I ask, "Do you know that there's more for you now?" I want to immediately plant a seed in their hearts and minds, and talk about the Holy Spirit. I want to simply explain to them what He can do in their lives.

A wonderful opportunity for pastors' wives is to take one evening a year and visit the Mpact Girls Clubs (formerly Missionettes). Just sit on the floor with the girls and tell them how you received the Holy Spirit and what He has done in your life. I have done this in churches we have pastored with wonderful results. At ten different times I've seen girls receive the Holy Spirit while we were all just sitting and praying. There may be other ladies in the church who would take on this ministry. I think the same approach would work with a man going into the Royal Rangers groups. This is one way our churches can start planting the seeds of hunger for the Baptism in our children. When are kids ever going to receive unless they are given an opportunity?

I like to see children receive early in life, but they need a personal coach (a parent or a Sunday School teacher) to teach them about what they have received, its importance, and why they need to speak in tongues. I like to tell young people how the power of the Holy Spirit kept me from a lot of sinful things teenagers can get into. I came through those years unscathed because the power of the Holy Spirit was in me and convicted me so that I immediately said no to sinful things.

On one occasion, I was sharing with a class of Missionettes and several girls were filled with the Holy Spirit. When their parents came to get them, the girls were still weeping and speaking in tongues. Some of their parents were not Christians and couldn't understand what was going on.

The next day, a lady approached me and said, "I'd like you to come and talk to us as mothers. We don't know what happened to our girls last night, and we need to understand."

My first feeling was that they were going to tear me apart. But when I prayed about it, the Lord said, "Just go and share your testimony. Share what the power of the Holy Spirit kept you from as a teenager." So that's what I did!

"Ladies," I said, "I can't tell you everything about the Holy Spirit, but I can tell you about my experience. I received such a love for God, and I received the power to say no to things that might have harmed me. My friends would be going another way and doing wrong things, but I was able to say no. The Holy Spirit kept me and held me, and gave me the power to be a leader instead of a follower."

Those five mothers sat there with tears streaming down their faces. They said, "That's what we want for our children."

I told them, "This is what your girls have received, and if they keep their prayer life strong and allow the Holy Spirit to convict and guide them, they will have the same experience as I did."

It opened their hearts and they realized that the Holy Spirit had not only touched their daughters' lives, but could make a difference in their lives as well.

PROCEDURE

Whenever we help someone seek the Baptism, the first step is to make sure things are right between the person and God. I always pray with them, asking God to reveal anything in their hearts that would hinder them from receiving the Holy Spirit.

When my dad was about nineteen years old, he wanted the Holy Spirit so badly. He prayed fervently for the Baptism. Every time he sat down and prayed, God would reveal to him things he had done. He was a rebellious teenager and would steal from people. As he prayed, whatever he had stolen would come to his mind. My dad said he knew the Holy Spirit was not going to fill him until he made things right. He did so and came back and told God, "My heart is ready and willing to be filled, and my life is clean." He was filled with the Holy Spirit.

Now, I know God does not expect someone to have every sin in his or her life perfectly worked out. There are some things God cleans up later; we don't have to be perfect. But if there are issues the Holy Spirit directs our minds to, we need to deal with them. Pray a prayer with anyone seeking the Baptism asking God to reveal anything in their heart and life that needs to be cleansed.

The second step is to explain to them that God's gift is just like a gift we give to our children at Christmas or on their birthday. Their name is written on that gift, and it's their gift if they will just receive it. They don't have to beg for it; they don't have to ask for it again and again. They simply have to receive it. This happens as they invite Jesus to fill them, and start praising and thanking Him for what He's done in their lives.

Thirdly, they have to take a step of faith by releasing their tongue to God as they praise. I often say, "You will get to the point where your tongue feels like it's too big for your mouth, and you want to say something. That is the Holy Spirit trying to say, 'Throw away your English and begin to speak in your heavenly language.'" That is when they need to take a step of faith and speak it—even if it feels funny to them.

Many times, they'll have stammering lips. I encourage them, "That is the Holy Spirit on you. Just step out by faith and begin to speak those words God has given you." For many years, I had stammering lips. No one ever told me I could use my tongue and lips to speak a beautiful language, or that it would become more beautiful as I spoke it.

Sometimes people just speak a few words and they stop. I encourage them to continue in prayer and use their heavenly, holy language. If there are people around them, I'll say, "Let's all speak in our heavenly language together." As the person uses his or her new, beautiful language, they don't feel like they're singled out. It gives them assurance that they have been filled.

I also tell them, "Tomorrow, when you begin to pray and the devil comes to you and says, 'You weren't filled with the Holy Spirit,' you just begin to pray in English and pour your heart out to God. You'll get to the point where the Holy Spirit will open you up so you can speak in your heavenly language."

Romans 8:26 says, "In the same way, the Spirit helps us in our weakness. We do not know what we ought to pray for, but the Spirit himself intercedes for us with groans that words cannot express." There are times when I don't know how to pray, but through the Holy Spirit, I can still pray the perfect prayer.

I went through cancer about four years ago. I didn't know at the time if my illness would be fatal, but I just began to pray in the Holy Spirit. I don't know what I was saying when I prayed in tongues, but I know I was praying in His perfect will. God then revealed to me I was going to live and He was going to use my sickness for His honor and glory. He was going to stretch me and use me in ways I had never been used before. This is often what the Holy Spirit will do for us.

DISCOURAGED SEEKERS

Sometimes I pray for people who have been seeking for many years, and they're already discouraged before they start to pray. My husband says, "Honey, this one's for you!" Just recently, a man came who had been seeking for many years, and I prayed with him for quite a long time before he received. I felt in my heart it was his night, and if I let him leave without being filled, he was going to feel like it was one more failure. Discouragement can really build up, so I kept encouraging him and praying with him until he was filled that night.

We have to keep the faith. Sometimes we almost have to have faith on behalf of the person we're praying with. He or she may say, "Well, maybe it's not for me." I reply, "No, we read in the Bible that this is for you, and your children, and your children's children. Why would God single you out and say 'It's not for you'?" The devil really takes advantage of discouragement.

CONCLUSION

When my husband was district superintendent, a young man came to him and said, "I'm a new Christian, but I need to receive the Holy Spirit. I keep praying and I can't. I just can't receive it." So my husband called to me and said, "Pray with this man. He needs the Holy Spirit." I told the man, "Just open your heart; I want you to receive it as a gift." I held his hands as a great, beautiful, heavenly language began to flow; it was instantaneous. He was shouting it! The whole place heard it! It was his appointed time, and I just happened to be there to encourage him.

Whether a church has classes on the baptism in the Holy

Spirit or a special Sunday night emphasis, we need to give opportunity for our people to be filled. The greatest way for them to want to be filled is by creating a hunger. Whenever we emphasize the Holy Spirit, people are filled. On one occasion, about fifty people were filled in a service. Bring someone in who can teach about the Holy Spirit, or take several Sunday nights and teach about it. But allow time for people to pray—and partner with them—that they may be filled with the Holy Spirit.

Remember that we are just one generation away from not being a Spirit-filled church.

CHAPTER SIX

FOSTERING A SETTING FOR PEOPLE TO RECEIVE

By Scott Erickson

There is work to be done to reach as many people with the gospel as possible before they go into eternity. This work can only be done effectively in the power of the Holy Spirit. I pray that as we consider these very important matters we would see the urgency of everyone in our churches experiencing the Baptism. Ministering the baptism in the Holy Spirit effectively involves several things including the right attitude, an appropriate atmosphere, and the anticipation that people will receive the gift. All these things can help create an environment that welcomes the work of the Holy Spirit.

ATTITUDE

The attitude of the person God will use to minister the Baptism is certainly one of enthusiasm—a person who is confident in the Word and in God's willingness to do what He promised. I am drawn to John 7:37,38 where Jesus teaches about the overflow and the fullness of the Spirit in a person's life.

If we think about that word "enthusiasm," we see it is built on the Greek, *en theos,* which means "in God." The mark of the truly enthused person is that God is in him or her. The picture in John 7 is of a person being so full of God that his or her behavior is dominated by the Spirit. Such a person inspires others to receive the baptism in the Holy Spirit. The enthusiastic, Spirit-filled Christian is dynamically alive and has something other people look at and say, "I really think that what you have is what I want."

Jesus spoke of these streams of living water during the Feast of the Tabernacles. Jesus called to everyone to come and enjoy the Spirit's fullness. He didn't speak of a little trickle of water. He said, "If anyone is thirsty, let him come to me and drink. Whoever believes in me, as the Scripture has said, streams of living water will flow from within him." (John 7:37,38). That deepened, fulfilling lifestyle comes from a life of the Spirit's overflow.

The attitude of a person who is ministering—whether it is a Sunday School teacher, pastor, or altar worker—must be assured God has a river of blessing He wants to pour out on people. We must be fully persuaded in our attitude to know that God is in the business of filling people with His Spirit and that the Spirit wants to abide in people in power. We must be persuaded that what the Bible says is true. There is no room for a vacillating presentation of Pentecost. We must be affirming, we must understand what to say and how to say it, we must be fully confident in what the Word says and what Jesus said about the Spirit.

Our attitude should be one of enthusiasm and also obedience. The baptism in the Holy Spirit is Christ's command to us, not a suggestion or an option. In Acts 1:4, Jesus "commanded them not to leave Jerusalem, but to wait for what the Father had promised" (NASB). We need to focus on the word "commanded," and realize it is very strong language. We must be fully persuaded that what God said in His Word is exactly what He meant.

We must also remember the role faith plays for the believer who is seeking the Baptism, and the importance of having an attitude of faith. If someone comes to the altar to receive the Holy Spirit while harboring doubt, Satan can use that doubt to prevent them from receiving the Holy Spirit. The believer must reject doubts and claim what God has promised. A person who yields to the Spirit will see God do great things in his or her life.

I was ministering to pastors in another country who were conducting Spirit-filled meetings but had not yet received the

Holy Spirit themselves. I asked them, "Would you just receive this gift by faith?" They said, "Well, we've been seeking this for a long time. We don't know why the Lord hasn't filled us." I explained to them that the gift has already been given, and it's just a matter of receiving it by faith. We shook hands, and then I prayed for them that they would receive the Spirit. There was no immediate sign and nothing physically occurred at that moment. But, after five or six years of seeking the Lord in this matter—it's an incredible thing—one pastor was baptized in the Spirit while he was preaching in his pulpit the next day!

Another man once came to me and said, "I've been seeking the Baptism for fifty-five years and I've been all over the country and had all kinds of people pray for me." He then talked to me about his faithful tithing and about all the works he had done. The Baptism has nothing to do with works; it has to do with faith.

"Can we just agree," I asked, "before I pray for you, that you're going to receive right now, and that you're not going to walk away from here and say, 'God didn't fill me,' but you will say, 'Today is the day I receive'?"

"Well, that's pretty direct," he said.

"It certainly is," I said.

I prayed for that man, and instantly he was speaking in other tongues. He looked like he had swallowed a light bulb! He was so filled with glory. To this day, although he is in his eighties, he is still enjoying a day-to-day Spirit-filled life. Attitude makes a difference.

ATMOSPHERE

In order for the Lord to respond and baptize people in His Spirit, we must create an atmosphere that is honoring to Him. The atmosphere God will honor is, first of all, an atmosphere of worship. Whether it is established at an altar, in someone's home, or in a Sunday School class, this atmosphere is one of complete and total wonder for the greatness of God; the Baptizer who is present needs to be honored. The minister needs to exercise whatever control is needed to make that atmosphere honorable to the Lord so the Spirit is not grieved in any way.

Many times we create an atmosphere of uncertainty. People don't know what to expect. An atmosphere conducive to the Baptism is one where a person understands what's going to happen and realizes what the Lord wants to do. I try to explain to people that they must understand Scripture and be properly prepared for what's about to happen.

I often point people to Acts 2:37,38: "When the people heard this, they were cut to the heart and said to Peter and the other apostles, 'Brothers, what shall we do?' Peter replied, 'Repent and be baptized, every one of you, in the name of Jesus Christ for the forgiveness of your sins. And you will receive the gift of the Holy Spirit.'" From this passage we understand the Baptism is a separate experience from salvation. We know that to be prepared to receive the Baptism we must first be born again.

I have prayed with people at the altar to receive salvation, and sometimes I have seen them filled with the Holy Spirit only seconds later—almost immediately upon their confession of Christ as Savior. As we think about creating the right atmosphere, we need to help people understand that they are not baptized with the Holy Spirit when they are born again. It doesn't happen in the same instant; salvation precedes the Baptism.

Let's look at the believers in Scripture who had not received the Baptism in the Holy Spirit. There are several examples:

> When the apostles in Jerusalem heard that Samaria had accepted the word of God, they sent Peter and John to them. When they arrived, they prayed for them that they might receive the Holy Spirit, because *the Holy Spirit had not yet come upon any of them*; they had simply been baptized into the name of the Lord Jesus. Then Peter and John placed their hands on them, and they received the Holy Spirit (Acts 8:14, emphasis added).

Here we see that believers had professed faith in Jesus, and in this case they had already been baptized in water, but they had not yet received the baptism in the Holy Spirit.

Consider also Acts 19:1–3:

> While Apollos was at Corinth, Paul took the road through the interior and arrived at Ephesus. There he found some disciples and asked them, 'Did you receive the Holy Spirit when you believed?' They answered, 'No, we have not even heard that there is a Holy Spirit.' So Paul asked, 'Then what baptism did you receive?' 'John's baptism,' they replied.

As we set the atmosphere for people to be spiritually ready, they must first receive Christ as Savior in order to receive the baptism in the Holy Spirit. Some may feel unworthy; some may feel they are not ready to be the kind of person who would have the Spirit flow in them in this way. But the atmosphere God honors is one in which truth abounds. If you are born again, you are ready to be filled with the Holy Spirit.

Because of Jesus' instruction to the disciples in Acts 1:4 to wait in Jerusalem until they had received power from on high, many people have assumed they also are required to tarry or wait. We do not wait in the same way as Jesus' first followers did because the Holy Spirit has already been given.

We need to consider the immediacy of how the Spirit fell in the New Testament. In Acts 8, for instance, the Bible says the Samaritans were immediately filled. In Acts 10:44, it says, "*While Peter was still speaking,*" the Spirit fell on all those in Cornelius's house "who heard the message" (emphasis added). Acts 19:1–6 gives clear reference to the Spirit baptizing believers "when Paul placed his hands on them." To set a correct atmosphere of expectation, we must remind people that the Spirit has already been given.

We must also remind people that the Holy Spirit baptism is a gift and is received by faith. I tell people they should expect to receive as hands are laid upon them. This creates a biblical expectancy. In Acts 8:17 and 19:6, believers received the Spirit as hands were laid upon them. Everything we receive from God is a gift we receive by faith. Without faith, we shouldn't think we're going to get anything from God (James 1:6,7). So we must create an atmosphere where people understand they must have faith that they will receive the gift of the Holy Spirit.

It is vitally important to remind people you're praying with that they are going to do the speaking. It may sound obvious, but in the Bible it was people who did the speaking in tongues when they received the Holy Spirit. They immediately spoke in other tongues, and we need to remind ourselves that we are going to do the talking when we receive the Baptism.

Of course, the Holy Spirit will give the utterance; we'll feel something in our vocal cords, our lips, and our tongue, and may not be certain what that feeling is. But we need to remember that Jesus does the baptizing and we do the speaking. Scripture says that He will enable us, and we will do the speaking.

Acts 10:44 says, "While Peter was still speaking these words, the Holy Spirit came on all who heard the message. The circumcised believers who had come with Peter were astonished that the gift of the Holy Spirit had been poured out even on the Gentiles. For they heard them speaking in tongues and praising God." They heard the Gentiles praying in other tongues.

We understand the good things the Spirit wants to do, and we need to learn how to deal with unbelief and allay the fears of the unknown. So we want to create an atmosphere that enables believers to understand they must cooperate with the Spirit. Luke 11:11–13 gives us a clear promise: "Which of you fathers, if your son asks for a fish, will give him a snake instead? Or if he asks for an egg, will give him a scorpion? If you then, though you are evil, know how to give good gifts to your children, how much more will your Father in heaven give the Holy Spirit to those who ask him!"

I usually mention that I've never seen a person filled with the Holy Spirit with their mouth closed. People need to relax, open their mouth and give praise to the Lord, and expect they will speak in a language they do not understand. The supernatural part is not who is doing the talking; it's what God is saying through us. We need to learn to lift our voice and trust God for the guidance. This creates an atmosphere of faith and worship, and God works in an atmosphere where people focus their attention on Him.

As people seek the Baptism, they feel very vulnerable. If someone is speaking one thing in one ear and someone else is speaking something else in the other ear, or people are crowded so closely they are in contact with those around them, it can really make people feel on edge.

ANTICIPATION

A lot of people seeking the Baptism are not sure what God is going to do. They may be very interested in knowing what God has for them, but they don't know what it is or what it looks like.

Philip's ministry in Samaria in Acts 8 intrigues me. Philip was preaching and good things were happening—miracles, signs, and wonders. The church in Jerusalem sent Peter and John to take part in Philip's ministry. In verse 17, when Peter and John laid their hands upon them "they received the Holy Spirit." I think we should pray, like Peter and John did, that people might receive the Holy Spirit, the gift God has already offered.

We can help people anticipate the Lord's promise by saying, "When I lay hands on you, I believe you're going to receive the Holy Spirit." In this way, we're creating in people a great sense of anticipation that what is said in God's Word is what we're going to do and what is going to happen.

God honors believers who have decided they will receive when someone lays hands on them. "When that pastor or that leader or that Sunday School teacher lays hands on me, I am going to receive the Holy Spirit." We must create an atmosphere built on the Word of God. Sometimes people feel unworthy and want to come to their own conclusions. We need to be people who simply say, "Lord, I know You know what my weakness is. I ask You to help me receive right now." We need to believe and anticipate with people that they can receive the gift of the Holy Spirit. God's gift of His Spirit is reserved for His children, and He desires for us to receive the Holy Spirit.

We must also remember the role faith plays for the candidate who is seeking the Baptism. If someone comes to the altar to receive the Holy Spirit while harboring doubts in their mind, or if they're thinking about how they were raised (perhaps in an anti-Pentecostal environment), Satan can use that doubt to prevent them from receiving the Holy Spirit. The believer must reject these doubts and claim what God has promised. A person who yields to the Spirit can know that God is going to do something great in their life.

Furthermore, the Holy Spirit wants to continue working in every person who has received the Baptism. We should not just emphasize that the Bible says the person who has been filled with the Holy Spirit will speak in other tongues. I believe the Bible also shows a new doorway for ministry that the Spirit-filled believer will experience. We should pray in tongues every day. Praying in the Spirit is a tremendous tool for our spiritual growth and empowerment. Along with the Word and the name of Jesus, praying in the Spirit daily keeps a person saturated in the love of God, keeps them refreshed, keeps their heart on fire and in tune with the Spirit, and enables them to see great things happen for the purposes of the Kingdom.

CHAPTER SEVEN

ENCOURAGEMENT IN RECEIVING THE GIFT

By Bill Juoni

We give follow-up instructions to new converts to help them understand what they have just experienced and to help them grow in their new life in Christ. It's just as important for us to give follow-up instructions to those who have been baptized in the Holy Spirit to help them understand what they have just experienced and to help them grow in what they have received and put it to use in their lives. We also need to encourage those we have prayed for who have not yet received the baptism in the Holy Spirit.

ENCOURAGEMENT FOR THOSE WHO HAVE RECEIVED

I share eight things with people after they have received the baptism in the Holy Spirit. These points will help them to continue living in the newfound power of the Baptism and make the most of what they have received.

1. *Speaking in tongues is the sign their experience is real.* Assure them if they were speaking in other tongues, they have received the baptism in the Holy Spirit. It doesn't matter what it sounded like or what they felt or what they did not feel. If they were speaking in other tongues, they have received the baptism in the Holy Spirit.

2. *They should not allow anyone to talk them out of what they have received.* Chances are, before the day is done the devil's going to whisper in their mind that they haven't received, or that they made all of it up, or that it wasn't God—it was their own words. They can't let the devil, or anyone else, talk them out of what they have experienced in God.

Christian friends who may not believe in the baptism in the Holy Spirit may try to talk them out of what they have experienced. There are many church fellowships that do not teach a Pentecostal experience for today. Believers themselves may have doubts about their experience, perhaps thinking it wasn't from God but rather their own imagination. No one should talk them out of what they've experienced in God—whether it's the devil, their friends, or even themselves.

When I received the baptism in the Holy Spirit, I was walking across a field on the campus of Northern Michigan University in Marquette. It was in the middle of the night, and nobody was around to share the experience with me. I went for weeks afterward doubting what I had experienced. It wasn't until a believer pulled me aside and encouraged me that I realized I really had received the Baptism.

3. *Emotions must not determine the reality of their experience.* The evidence of the baptism in the Holy Spirit, according to Scripture, is that the believer spoke in other tongues. The evidence is not what he or she felt or the emotions that were or were not displayed.

People's feelings vary dramatically. Some people who are baptized in the Holy Spirit—in addition to speaking in other tongues—will have tears coming down their cheeks. Others may shake. Others may feel like they've been hit with a bolt of lightning. Others may describe a quiet, peaceful feeling—no tears, no shaking, no falling down—nothing besides speaking in tongues appeared to happen. However, the reality of what people experience is not based on what they do or do not feel. The evidence is speaking in other tongues.

4. *After receiving the Baptism, believers should pray in the Holy Spirit every day; they should put to use what they have received.*

In Ephesians 6:18, Paul says, "Pray in the Spirit on all occasions with all kinds of prayers and requests. With this in mind, be alert and always keep on praying for all the saints." Encourage believers who have received the Baptism to pray in the Holy Spirit every day. Paul, writing in Romans 8:26, said, "In the same way, the Spirit helps us in our weakness. We do not know what we ought to pray for, but the Spirit himself intercedes for us with groans that words cannot express." Believers who take time every day to pray in the Spirit will receive help from Him in their communion with God.

5. *The number of words used, or even how one's prayer language sounds, is unimportant.* The key is to put our prayer language to use and to take time to pray in the Spirit every day.

I was with a pastor some time ago in Minnesota. "You know," he said, "when I was baptized in the Holy Spirit, I think I spoke one word."

What's wrong if someone is praying with one word? Perhaps the Spirit is helping that person say "thank you" to God in another language or "help" to God in another language. As believers use what they have been given, it will grow and develop in their lives.

6. *The Baptism is not an end in itself, or something to check off on a spiritual "to do" list.* Some may feel, "Well, now I've received this, and I can just kind of push it aside and forget about it."

The Baptism is just the beginning of a new dimension in the life of a believer. He or she now has new power in life—a new way to pray, a new way to worship God, a new way to be strengthened, and a whole host of other benefits. This isn't the end of something; it's just the beginning.

7. *The Baptism's power is to be put to use in all of life.* Baptized believers should step out in faith as opportunities arise and the Holy Spirit opens doors and nudges them.

I compare the baptism in the Holy Spirit to the passing gear on a car. As you're driving along, you don't even really know that the passing gear is there. Then, as you go to pass another car, you press on the gas pedal and that passing gear kicks in when there's a need and when there's a purpose for it.

As we step out in faith—whether to tell someone about Jesus, pray for someone, or be used in the gifts of the Holy Spirit—the empowerment from the baptism in the Holy Spirit will also kick in, just like the passing gear. As we put this new power to use and step out in faith as opportunities arise, we'll find this power will enable us to minister in whatever way God wants us to minister.

8. *It's normal to have questions about the Baptism experience.* When questions arise, the believer should feel free to express them. Encourage believers not to harbor questions. It's normal to have questions and it's best to ask them of a well-respected, Spirit-filled believer.

ENCOURAGEMENT FOR THOSE WHO HAVE NOT YET RECEIVED

It is also a reality when we pray with people to receive the baptism in the Holy Spirit that not all will receive immediately. In fact, the only person who has never experienced praying for someone who did not receive the Baptism immediately is probably the person who has never prayed for anyone to receive the Baptism in the first place.

I heard an old-time Pentecostal preacher say there are two reasons people don't receive the Baptism—it's either a lack of faith (they don't believe they can receive) or it's a lack of submission (they do not yield their mouth, tongue, mind and heart, thus not allowing God to do in them what He is waiting to do if they would yield themselves).

I share four things with individuals who have not received the Baptism in the hope it will encourage them.

1. *God loves them.* We all need the assurance that God loves us, especially when we have asked Him for the gift of the Holy Spirit baptism and have not yet received it. Just because someone has not yet received, it does not mean God loves him or her any less.

2. *God wants to baptize them in the Holy Spirit.* God wants to baptize them in the Holy Spirit even more than they want to receive the Baptism.

3. *They must keep seeking.* The believer must not quit or give up in despair. He or she must keep seeking and desiring to be baptized in the Holy Spirit.

4. *They must stay open to the baptism in the Holy Spirit as God's promise.* It's easy to allow discouragement to shut down one's faith in God's unchanging promise. If the person remains hungry, at some point God's faithfulness will be expressed in the Baptism.

I often share stories of when I prayed for people to be baptized in the Holy Spirit and they didn't receive at the altar, but they stayed open and hungry and received later. One girl went back to pick up her Bible and started speaking in other tongues at the back pew. There have been people who have been baptized in the Holy Spirit on their way home from church, some at their bedside, some in the shower the next morning.

As people stay open and hungry, the promise from Scripture is that they will be baptized in the Holy Spirit. If someone didn't receive when you prayed for them, it's not the end of the world. It does not mean God doesn't want to fill them. God will baptize them in the Holy Spirit. They just need to stay open, stay hungry, and keep seeking until He does.

ENCOURAGEMENT FOR PASTORS

I want to encourage pastors to keep on ministering on the baptism in the Holy Spirit, and keep on giving opportunities for people to receive. As you consistently give opportunities, people will be filled with the Holy Spirit.

Having been a pastor for twenty years, I know where you're coming from. Sometimes your voice is too familiar to the people. Have someone come in from the outside, a new voice saying it in a little different way. People respond who may normally not have responded.

While our kids were growing up, there were times I would say something to them and it was like water off a duck's back. Three weeks later, they'd come bursting through the door talking about something a neighbor had said. It was basically the same thing I had said to them, just a little different wording and from a different voice. Yet my kids talked about it like it was the greatest revelation they had ever heard! Sometimes, I think a pastor can find himself dealing with that same kind of situation and mindset.

I also encourage you to incorporate teaching on the Baptism into the teaching of the church. Start with your new believers class. That is an excellent place to introduce people to the baptism in the Holy Spirit. When sharing the fundamental beliefs of the church, include a segment dealing with the Baptism. This holds true for membership classes and Bible studies.

Preach the Baptism as well. People aren't going to be able to receive the Baptism unless you're preaching on it and giving them opportunities to receive. I say that because I was asking the Lord one day why people were not being baptized in the Holy Spirit in our church. The Lord basically said, "Well, you're not giving them a chance." That's when I realized I needed to preach on the Baptism and give people a chance to receive.

In our first pastorate, we had a time after worship when people could come forward for prayer, regardless of their need. Week after week, we began to notice that people were coming forward because they wanted to receive the baptism in the Holy Spirit. I wasn't even preaching on it, but they were coming forward to receive the Baptism during that altar call.

I finally asked, "Why are all these people coming forward?" I found out one of the Sunday School classes was teaching on the Baptism. People were getting the teaching in their Sunday School class and coming forward to receive the Baptism during an altar time in main service, even when I wasn't preaching on it. They were hungry to be filled with the Holy Spirit!

A little lightbulb went off in my head. Hey, if we teach on this at all, even if we're not preaching on it at that time, people are going to come forward wanting to be filled with the Holy Spirit.

Be intentional. Don't get discouraged. Keep standing with those people in your congregation who have yet to experience the Baptism. God will honor His promise.

CHAPTER EIGHT

THE HOLY SPIRIT AND SMALL GROUPS

By Randy Valimont

It is my joy and privilege to pastor First Assembly of God in Griffin, Georgia, and to be part of a Fellowship committed to a living Pentecost. We emphasize the baptism in the Holy Spirit at every opportunity, and in every expression of our church's ministry. Why? Because the Baptism is God's promised enduement of power to help believers witness and share their faith in Christ Jesus. This is the mission of the church, both worldwide and locally.

The Baptism is a very personal experience, and some churches find it a challenge to teach about and encourage a congregation to seek the Baptism in a public setting. Although a Pentecostal body of believers should never feel uncomfortable promoting the Baptism in a large setting, there are many other venues in which believers can be baptized in the Spirit.

We encourage people in their Sunday School classes and an array of small groups to give regular invitations to seek and experience the baptism in the Holy Spirit. We tell our teachers and small group leaders that every time they gather they should give an invitation for salvation and an invitation to receive the Baptism.

You can observe this dynamic in Scripture. When Peter shared the gospel in the household of Cornelius, those who heard were baptized in the Spirit (Acts 10:44–46). When Paul visited a small group of brethren in Ephesus, he led them into receiving the Baptism (Acts 19:1–7).

People often feel less threatened in a small group and more at home. They are more receptive when people they know are there, laying hands on them and praying with them in a nonconfrontational way. The small group setting is a setting based on relationship. Small groups, then, are a perfect environment for receiving this gift of the Spirit intended to deepen the believer's relationship with God and empower Christians to share the good news relationally.

PREPARED TO LEAD

Whether in the larger congregational setting or in a small group, those serving in ministry must be prepared to lead others into the Baptism. Peter and Paul were not mere theorists when they communicated the vitality of the Holy Spirit infilling to their respective audiences. Peter was gloriously filled on the Day of Pentecost and empowered to preach to the Jerusalem multitude (Acts 2), and he was later filled when standing before the Jewish religious leaders (Acts 4:8–12). Paul's experiences in the Spirit were such that he could write to the Corinthian church "I speak in tongues more than all of you" (1 Corinthians 14:18). This was certainly no prideful boast, but rather a reflection on Paul's deep commitment to Pentecost in his own life.

Leaders who are praying over people in their small groups or in their Sunday School classes must feel comfortable and confident in doing so. Without that confidence, there will be a lack of faith and enthusiasm when praying for someone to receive, if there is any prayer offered at all. In order to help group leaders at our church understand this kind of prayer as a natural extension of their group ministry, we ask them to stand with our pastoral staff at the altar during church services and pray for people to receive the baptism in the Holy Spirit. Once leaders become accustomed to praying for people to receive the Baptism in a larger church setting, they are ready and at ease when praying with people in a small group setting.

Before the moment of prayer arrives, leaders first need to understand how to encourage a believer to seek the Baptism. Here are four basic things to emphasize.

First, leaders should be able to give simple instruction on the need for and purpose of the Baptism. Every believer should understand what the baptism in the Holy Spirit is, what He does, and what the enduement of power is for.

Second, leaders should know the appropriate questions to ask each person in their group: "Have you accepted Jesus as your Savior?" or "Is there anything in your life you need to give to the Lord so you can be free to receive everything He has for you?"

Third, train leaders to pray in faith. It is just as important to pray in faith as you pray over someone to receive the baptism in the Holy Spirit as it is to pray in faith when you're praying for someone who is sick. Likewise, it should be no harder to receive the baptism in the Holy Spirit than it is to receive Jesus as Savior.

Fourth, leaders should be a spiritual resource for the seeker. They need to encourage the seeker that the Baptism is their experience for the asking, even if it does not occur immediately. It is a promised gift from God, and until the seeker receives this gift, the leader will be available and ready to offer help, ministry and encouragement. The person who does not receive the Baptism right away needs to know there are others willing to stand with him or her.

It remains the priority of our Sunday School leaders and small group leaders to make sure everyone in their group is born again. But part and parcel of the teaching on salvation is further teaching on the Baptism. We want everyone in each of our group settings to understand what the baptism in the Holy Spirit is, what the Spirit does, and how He will function in their lives.

Every one of our group leaders is baptized in the Holy Spirit and has at one time or another prayed with someone and seen him or her filled with the Spirit. This is a core requirement for anyone who serves as a small group leader at First Assembly. No leader can take people in a spiritual direction they have never been.

READY TO RECEIVE

A leader who is prepared to offer strong biblical teaching on the Baptism as well as partner with the seeker in prayer is still only half of the equation. The person seeking the Baptism must be ready as well.

It may seem like an obvious point, but it should be clearly stated anyway: the seeker must have a clearly identified salvation experience. It is entirely possible for a person to be seeking the Baptism simply because it seems to be the thing to do in a Pentecostal church, when all along they are attending that church without a foundational relationship with Christ.

Second, the seeker must be hungry for the Baptism. This is not a casual pursuit for any believer. It is fundamental to a believer's participation in the Great Commission and experiencing God's power in life to effectively impact other lives.

Third, the seeker will know he or she has received the Holy Spirit when there is initial physical evidence—speaking in other tongues. Leaders need to talk to their groups about the prayer language that comes from the Holy Spirit.

Fourth, seekers should understand that the Baptism is not a cookie-cutter experience. God created us with wonderful variety, and there is wonderful variety in how He sends His Spirit. Some people receive the Baptism loudly, and some people receive it softly. I've seen people laugh as they speak in tongues. We teach our leaders not to put people in a proverbial box but to let the Holy Spirit minister to people as He chooses.

Leaders and group members must remember that the Holy Spirit baptism can occur in any setting. I've heard of people receiving the Holy Spirit in their car while driving to work or going to school. I know of a schoolteacher who had been fasting, wanting to receive the Holy Spirit. At a break between classes, she went into the break room by herself. While she was reading her Bible, she began to worship the Lord and say simple, sincere phrases like, "Lord, I love You." As she began to talk with the Lord in this heartfelt manner, all of a sudden she was baptized in the

Holy Spirit and began to speak in other tongues right there during public school as she was taking a break.

Our small group settings allow for these kinds of testimonies to be shared and for more personal teaching on the Baptism to occur. We train our leaders and offer our small groups with the constant goal of making sure people understand the importance of the Baptism, understand how to receive the Baptism, and understand that wherever they connect within the church, they will encounter time and room for the Spirit of God to move in their lives.

POSITIONED FOR BLESSING

Once you have leaders trained to teach and pray on the Baptism, and group members who are acting on opportunities to receive the Baptism, you may ask, "What are the dynamics for the group setting itself?"

Small groups are not as constrained by a time schedule. There is greater flexibility than with the time restrictions of a church service or even in a Sunday School setting. Small groups allow for more time for people to receive the individual attention they might need as they seek the Baptism.

The proper atmosphere is important as well. I'm not suggesting there is only one atmosphere anymore than I am saying there is only one way to receive the Baptism. But some basic factors create a setting conducive to a Pentecostal infilling.

In every small group there should be worship. Some of our small groups have live music, some play a CD of worship music, but there is worship in each small group. Worship is vitally important; it opens a person's spirit to receive every blessing God would bestow. When people are worshipping the Lord, there is a more natural environment for that worship to transition into speaking in tongues. When people receive the baptism in the Holy Spirit, in my experience, it has been a result of hunger and thirst for the Lord and being in His presence. I can't think of a better way to get into the presence of the Lord than to begin to love

Him with expressions of worship and praise.

We instruct our leaders to encourage their groups to seek the Baptism by opening with a brief time to get the people's minds focused on the things of heaven, and begin to worship Jesus. As that focused worship begins to happen, leaders can transition the group into welcoming the Spirit of God to have liberty in their lives.

When I teach on these dynamics, some have argued with me that taking such steps is really a form of manipulation. I do not believe it is manipulation, but rather atmosphere. God created an intangible atmosphere that surrounds us and gives us every breath for our survival. The physical atmosphere sustains life. When people seek to receive the baptism in the Holy Spirit, they need to make a spiritual transition into an atmosphere of heaven, where heaven's values and priorities are welcomed and the power of the Holy Spirit is welcomed. That invitation takes place when people are worshipping God and their lives are attuned to His presence.

We have small groups that meet in Sunday School and small groups that meet in homes. Usually, people who go to a Sunday School class don't go to a home group, and the people who go to a home group don't go to a Sunday School class. With this exercise of personal preference in mind, we try to make sure there is a balance at each location, and that we give opportunity for those who are there to receive the baptism in the Holy Spirit.

Our home group settings vary widely. A number of our groups are built around a common interest of the members, such as motorcycles. But even in this setting we teach our leaders, at some point during the activity, to share a brief devotional. When it comes to helping members to seek and receive the Baptism, we encourage leaders to periodically offer some kind of spiritual retreat—a special day or weekend gathering when members can seek the Spirit. We supply curriculum and a fifteen-minute teaching DVD.

The bottom line is this: even people who join a group for a special interest will encounter teaching and encouragement on the Baptism. No one should have to transfer to another group in order to receive the Holy Spirit.

PART OF A WHOLE

Small groups are experiencing a growing presence in many Assemblies of God churches. But no church should lose sight of its larger, corporate identity. While there are wonderful benefits to presenting Spirit baptism in the smaller context of a Sunday School class or home group, the Holy Spirit wants to move powerfully over the entire congregation when it gathers. There is a big picture here—one of full integration and a comprehensive Pentecostal emphasis throughout the church.

The Baptism is a core value we emphasize on Sunday morning, Sunday night, Wednesday night, and during Sunday School classes and small groups. We are an unapologetically Pentecostal church. That is who we are. We accept our mandate from Christ himself to win people who are lost. We recognize we need that empowering presence of the Spirit to accomplish that mission. And when people are saved, we want everyone in our fellowship to receive the baptism in the Holy Spirit so they, too, can reach out with the gospel

We want everyone to be a soul winner, and to be the best soul winner you can possibly be, you must be filled with the Holy Spirit. There is no age limit to this gift. We have a video of twenty-two of our children in children's church receiving the Baptism and speaking in tongues. Their baptism in the Holy Spirit was so compelling we showed the video to our church. The congregation went wild with excitement and praise. Why? Because they saw that in every area—whether it's Royal Rangers, MPact Girls Clubs (formerly Missionettes), Sunday School, children's church, or small groups—the value to the church of being Spirit-filled is recognized and the Baptism is fervently sought.

The Holy Spirit has brought about our church's vitality and growth as well as our community impact. We believe He desires to do even greater miracles among us.

CHAPTER NINE

LEADING A RECEIVING TIME

By Tim Enloe with others

The thought of leading a receiving time could start a spiritual panic attack for some! Leaders can easily struggle with fears when it comes to bringing others into what we have experienced ourselves. After all, it's not as if we're teaching them algebra or how to build a birdhouse; there are no pat formulas or recipes that guarantee success every time. We're simply trying to help others receive a supernatural experience that cannot be fully understood by natural processes.

The following comments are for those who will lead a small group receiving time or church altar service. Your responsibility and attitude should be the same regardless of the venue.

BE A LEADER

The outcome of a receiving time can be determined by a leader's sense of responsibility. If a leader tries to shoulder the responsibility for everyone in the room to receive—and gauges his or her personal worth on that indicator—he or she can be overwhelmingly discouraged. On the other hand, a leader who throws all of the responsibility on the people and is proud, cavalier, or desensitized to others' feelings can inflict much damage on seekers.

I preached my first sermon when I was sixteen to a group at a retirement center. I was scared to death and couldn't figure out what to preach about until my dad gave me his usual dose of wise counsel, "Do you know what God wants to accomplish in the service?" he asked. "If you can find that out and then preach about it, it will happen." That may sound overly pragmatic, but the advice has served me well over the years. You have been directed by God to minister on this subject, so do it! It will happen.

We often feel more comfortable in leading others to understanding (teaching/preaching) than we do in leading them into experiencing (receiving). After all, the first is concrete and the second seems more abstract. But we must help people both understand and experience this gift by leading them to the Baptizer and letting Him do the miracle in their lives.

As leaders, our responsibility is not to "get people Spirit baptized," but rather, to lead people to the place where they can receive. Our goal is for people to encounter the presence and power of the Holy Spirit in a new and often dramatic way.

Ken Cramer adds:

> Comprehension brings alignment. If you teach about the Spirit baptism so that seekers can comprehend it, they will begin to align themselves so that they're ready to receive. They can say, "I see it in the Word and I'm ready for Him to take me to the next level." The number one problem resulting in disappointed seekers is ministers who strong-arm a response rather than instruct from the Word and let the Spirit do the rest. Once people wrap their minds around what God is making available to them by the baptism in the Spirit, you won't be able to chase them away from receiving Him.

Sometimes our own problems can hinder us from being the spiritual leader we need to be. Allen Griffin addresses how we can overcome this obstacle to spiritual leadership:

> I believe that the most important consideration when leading an altar service is personal preparation. Many times ministers or altar workers

can find themselves in difficult and even strange situations if they are not prepared to minister with clean hands and a pure heart. I know this might sound trivial, but it is not. Being sidetracked by personal issues, insecurities, and sin can derail even the most powerful altar services. We must deal with our personal issues and problems and let them be settled. Then the Lord will enable us to move on in ministry.

The altar service is about the seeker, not us. How we feel and our stories of tragedy or triumph can only misalign our purpose. Keep the subject matter and attention on those who are seeking. Fasting and prayer get us personally and corporately prepared to minister to others and open lines of communication for God to speak through us. Allowing ourselves to be emptied of selfishness gives us the ability to be ready for God's use. Praying God's Word is much more valuable than a story or anecdote of our own experience that may or may not apply to a seeker's situation.

BE AN ENCOURAGER

I often direct my comments to encourage seekers during the process of receiving. I try to let them know that their concerns and thoughts are normal. For instance, I may say, "If you've been praying for a while and you have not been filled, there's nothing wrong with you. Sometimes it just takes a while to receive." This type of comment can "reset" frustrated seekers who may feel that they are doing something wrong and therefore can't receive. A few appropriate (and appropriately timed) words of encouragement during the receiving time can keep seekers focused and hungry.

Randy Hurst reemphasizes how critical the faith factor is in receiving:

> Holy Spirit baptism is a gift that is received by faith. I believe people's faith can be helped and that each person's faith is unique. In my younger years, I remember people who had a special gift of faith to join with someone else's to receive. A person praying with others to

receive needs discernment to know when praying with them encourages their faith and when it interferes. When Jesus taught us that if two agree on anything it will be given/done, that also applies to the Holy Spirit baptism. Join your faith to others. But remember, as Tim Enloe says in chapter one, some people find it easier to receive if they are praying alone.

Bill Juoni offers some sound encouragement to seekers during these times:

> I always share two practical points with those seeking the baptism in the Holy Spirit. In order for us to speak in any language, whether English or tongues, we need to open our mouth, move our tongue, and speak. If we don't open our mouth and move our tongue, we won't be able to speak anything. But as we open our mouth and move our tongue, God will then give us words in that new language.

The first time I sought to receive the baptism in the Holy Spirit, I wasn't filled because I was at the altar with my teeth clenched and my jaw locked. A few weeks later I received the baptism in the Holy Spirit while walking across a field in the middle of the night. I was praying out loud, asking the Lord to baptize me in the Holy Spirit. It happened quickly and easily. The key was that my mouth was open, my tongue was already moving, and all the Lord had to do was give me the words.

Second, no one can speak two languages at the same time. Only one language can come out of one mouth at one time. Before praying for people to be baptized in the Holy Spirit, I encourage them to join me in worshipping the Lord together out loud in English. Then I tell them that after a few moments I am going to pray a simple prayer and ask the Lord to baptize them in the Holy Spirit. When I pray that simple prayer, they need to stop worshipping in English and begin to speak in the language the Lord is giving them. It will sound strange to them, but all new languages sound strange. Unless they stop speaking in English, however, they will not be able to speak in tongues. Sometimes I'll have to ask people to stop speaking in English, take a deep breath, and then speak the language the Lord is giving to them.

Dick Gruber offers this specific insight to encourage children during a receiving time:

> Be positive! God wants to fill every child to overflowing. Encourage children to ask God for this gift according to Luke 11:13.
>
> Once they have asked God for His baptism in the Spirit, encourage them to praise and glorify God out loud. In twenty-five years of praying with children, I have never witnessed a child receive this gift without first praising God out loud in his or her native tongue.
>
> Never tell a child that he or she has received. Ask them what God is doing. Ask if they are speaking in tongues. If the answer is yes, encourage them to continue. Remind children that according to Luke 11:13, those who ask will receive. Encourage them to speak out by faith when the Holy Spirit gives them even a partial word to say.

Allen Griffin adds: "Smile at kids when you pray. Children think something is wrong when we go to God in 'anger.' A calm demeanor sets them at ease and lets them get ready for God to do something good."

Seeking the Holy Spirit baptism can easily be incorporated into a youth or young adult setting as well.

Judi Bullock says:

> In a small group setting, I usually try to share my testimony of when and how I was filled at nine years of age. I tell them how the Holy Spirit has helped me live the Christian life and enabled me to be an overcomer. His power works in and through us to give us the strength to say no to wrong choices and yes to God's will. When we are going through hard trials and troubles, we can rely on the Spirit since He helps us to pray the perfect prayer for every situation.
>
> I explain that we must present to God a heart that is cleansed from sin and wanting all that He has. After this, I simply ask if they would like to receive the Holy Spirit. We begin praising God and thanking Him for who He is and what He has done. We ask Him for the gift of the Holy Spirit, which He is so willing to give.

BE A LISTENER

Leading a time when the supernatural can happen is all about listening to the Holy Spirit. We live in a culture where everyone is afraid of silence or "dead air," but listening to the Holy Spirit is often much easier when you are quiet. As one of my elementary teachers often said, "You can't listen when you are talking."

A mistake I have frequently made involves listening to music during a receiving time rather than the Holy Spirit. Often we can get so caught up in the worship music that it becomes more of the main focus than the purpose of receiving. If you listen to the Spirit, He'll show you what to do in those moments. Perhaps you need to ask the worship team to play quiet instrumental music for a few minutes. God will direct you if you listen.

Randy Hurst adds:

> In a recent interview with Dr. George Wood for his book on core values, he comments on this: "A very important factor in a receiving time is that the atmosphere not be distracting from someone's personal seeking. Unfortunately, sometimes worship teams can be singing so loudly that people struggle to focus on their prayers during an altar time. I honestly miss times of prayer around the altar when only soft piano or organ music was playing."

It is amazing how naturally the Lord will guide you step-by-step if you will trust Him. He usually speaks just enough information to get the job done and usually speaks just as you need to know it. Remember, He wants to see seekers empowered even more than you and I do!

Once you've presented a simple teaching on Spirit baptism and invited a response, pause and listen for His voice. He just might drop some divine wisdom into your natural understanding.

Probably the easiest mistake a leader can make is to ignore the needs of the people they are called to serve. I have often misunderstood what people really were going through because I didn't stop to listen to them.

Pastor Ken Cramer explains this so well:

> When you are conducting a seeking time for the Baptism, remember that there could be any number of reasons people answer the altar call. They may be there because they just came through a difficult breakup, a family member may have died and they are looking for God's help, or they need a job. Don't assume they are there for the reason you gave in the altar call. A simple question such as, "What would you like Jesus to do for you?" or "What are you expecting God to do right now?" will help you understand what they are thinking. As every flight attendant says before the plane leaves the gate, "If your travel plans don't include (destination city), you might want to get off this plane."

Pentecostal altar calls should be noted for the evidence that God is there working among His people. At times people have been so noisy that it is difficult to find God. Many seekers find themselves overwhelmed by the clutter of instructions from well-meaning bystanders. It's time to unclutter our altar times.

If there are enough well-instructed prayer counselors, let one seeker and one counselor pray together. If there are many more seekers than altar workers, let one worker lead the entire group and others lend support.

Listening at altar time is critical! This is when the workers help seekers navigate around hindrances, words of knowledge flow, and practical instructions are given. Be careful not to get "swept away" in emotion and become a distraction for the people still seeking. When everyone has received, that is the time to shout and celebrate as one voice for the fantastic outpouring that God just gave.

When praying with children, don't pray in a spiritual language around them until after they have received their own. In this way they take ownership in what God has done for them and they aren't tempted to copy someone else.

When people receive the fullness of the Spirit in a setting free of "emotional clutter," they have a greater understanding of what God has done and will be more capable of sharing it with others. If God's Spirit took chaos and made order at the creation of the universe, He'll help us move an altar time from clutter to clarity.

TAKE YOUR TIME

I am convinced that the most overlooked ingredient in leading a receiving time is just that: time. If you give the Holy Spirit time to move, He will.

You may be concerned that no one will stay for the prayer time. I've found that a simple explanation goes a long way. Before every receiving session, I try to give an explanation, such as: "We're going to learn about the Holy Spirit's power from the Bible, then we are going to take some time—twenty or thirty minutes (or more!), praying to receive His power. Don't miss the prayer time at the end of the service; it is the best part! You can actually experience the Holy Spirit's power for yourself." People will stay and receive.

You may notice that the Holy Spirit will often move in waves with a calm period between. Patience at the altar pays off.

Allen Griffin says:

> Leading an altar service requires tenacity. Altar ministry is not for the timid. When brothers and sisters come to the altar seeking an encounter with God, we must allow them to see passion and dynamic (but true to character) excitement exuding from our spirit. Our expectation of the Spirit's moving and direction is infectious and will help prepare hearts before we lay one hand on one head or recite any Scriptures. There may be tears, so grab a hanky and keep going! Press in with people in meekness and hunger. Our attitude affects our altitude.
>
> Don't be alarmed if the fire doesn't fall from heaven immediately. Allow people to open up and give God time to move as He pleases. I frequently say, "Don't get in a hurry; just slow down and enjoy His presence."

*All quoted material in this chapter comes from personal communication between author and person being quoted.

CHAPTER TEN

THE HOLY SPIRIT BAPTISM AND CHILDREN

By Dick Gruber

For more than thirty years I have been involved in children's church, crusades, and children's camps. I have witnessed to, led, and prayed for hundreds of children as they received the baptism in the Holy Spirit. I have seen this gift distributed freely among boys and girls as young as four and five years old. I have stood by as children prayed for other children and spoke words of wisdom to help their friends understand and receive this unique gift. In this writing, I will share with you some practical insights on leading children into the baptism in the Holy Spirit.

I interviewed more than one hundred children a few years back while speaking at a statewide children's camp. Not one of them could tell me about the baptism in the Holy Spirit. Only two had ever heard of speaking with other tongues. It was as if I had been transported to the setting of Acts 19 and was standing alongside Paul as the Ephesians believers told him, "We have not even heard that there is a Holy Spirit" (Acts 19:2). By Thursday night of that week most of those children could not only explain what the baptism in the Holy Spirit was, but they had also experienced this wonderful gift.

So how did that happen? What approach did I take at those altars? When do you know it is the right time to pray? Let's look at these and other questions so we can better understand how to lead children in this important aspect of Christian living.

LET THE CHILDREN LEARN

We want our children to experience the best quality teaching when it comes to the basics of reading, writing, and arithmetic. We do what we can to insure that our school systems provide well-trained, pleasant teachers who make learning a joy for the young ones. Then the kids come to church. Do they deserve less than the best on Sunday mornings? Children must have competent people of good character training them in biblical truths. Children need solid, interesting teaching when it comes to spiritual matters. In no other spiritual aspect is this more important than the baptism in the Holy Spirit.

So how do you, as the children's teacher or leader, approach this subject? First, look to the Bible. What does it say about this gift and about children receiving it? In Acts 1:5, Jesus said, "For John baptized with water, but in a few days you will be baptized with the Holy Spirit." It is important for children to know Jesus used the term "baptized" when referring to this second gift. We are talking about a promise of God.

In Luke 11, when teaching on prayer, Jesus uses an illustration any child can understand. "Which of you fathers, if your son asks for a fish, will give him a snake instead? Or if he asks for an egg, will give him a scorpion? If you then, though you are evil, know how to give good gifts to your children, how much more will your Father in heaven give the Holy Spirit to those who ask him!" (Luke 11:11–13). I have used this simple illustration many times to assure children that when they ask God sincerely for this gift He will not allow them to fake it or receive a counterfeit. I also use this passage to encourage children to ask God for this gift in the first place.

I usually include Acts 2:39 when talking with children about this gift. It reads, "The promise is for you and your children and for all who are far off—for all whom the Lord our God will call." Even if you choose to generalize the word "children" in this passage, you cannot ignore the context that it would include all believers, both young and old, throughout history.

It is important, when teaching children, to incorporate all of the senses. While speaking the Word will have impact, causing it to come alive using everyday objects helps clarify for children. I have developed several teachings using everyday objects when discussing the baptism in the Holy Spirit with children. Here are two that work well: "The Bike" and "The Kid's Meal."

The Bike

Place an ordinary child's bicycle in front of the children. I turn it upside down, standing it on the handlebars and seat. Invite a child to come to the front of the room and assist you. I place a bike helmet on that child and talk about the helmet of salvation. Just as a bike rider must wear a helmet as he rides, the child must be saved before seeking the baptism in the Holy Spirit. This is a gift reserved for those who believe. The Ephesians of Acts 19 listened to Paul, accepted the Word, and were baptized in water showing their newfound commitment to Christ, and then hands were laid on them to receive the Holy Spirit.

My child assistant is then instructed to point to the front tire while turning the pedals and thus empowering the rear tire. I talk about the Baptism being like a bike. A bicycle comes with two tires, front and rear. The front tire gives the ride balance and direction. This is what a prayer language does. The back tire gives power to move forward. Again, this is what the power of the Holy Spirit does for the believer.

Nobody would think of trying to ride a bike that was missing a tire. Just as the bike has a front and rear tire, the baptism in the Holy Spirit provides the believer with power and a prayer language. Every time a child rides a bike or sees someone riding, he can remember the blessing of the baptism in the Holy Spirit.

Receiving is as simple as riding a bike. At first you may use training wheels or receive encouragement from a parent or older sibling. When receiving the Holy Spirit, you may use the training wheels of verbal praise by receiving encouragement from a friend or pastor to speak out praises to God.

Once a believer has received power and a prayer language as the Spirit baptized him, he or she should be sure to use that gift every day. Nobody would buy a brand-new bike and park it in the garage all year. A child with a bike will ride it every chance he gets. He would not save it to ride one week a summer or only on special days. A bike gives a boy or girl freedom. The Baptism will do the same, giving a child freedom to grow into a deeper walk with God.

The Kid's Meal

Purchase any kid's meal from a fast food restaurant. I bring five children up front and allow each to hold a different part of the kid's meal. I take a little time to talk about each part and compare it to an aspect of the baptism in the Holy Spirit. I then remind all of the children to remember these things when they eat a kid's meal. This lesson includes the following components:

- The bag or box represents the Bible, which holds all we know about the Holy Spirit.
- The prize represents speaking in tongues. Most people go for this prize first.
- The meat represents the power of the Holy Spirit, received when the believer is baptized in the Holy Spirit.
- The fries are like the extra gifts, like prophecy or tongues and interpretation.
- The fountain drink represents the joy of the Lord.

Be certain to explain fully what will happen when you pray with the children for this gift. I have found many children to be afraid of the unknown. They do not break through in prayer because of a hidden fear. Sometime in my presentation about this gift I address fears children may have.

Some of those fears expressed to me by children include uncontrollable tongue talking, blacking out, being shaken by adult workers, or prophetic information coming into their brain like an explosion. One girl mentioned she was afraid of praying because she might get slain in the Spirit and hit her head on the floor. I encouraged her to go ahead and just lie down. That way, if God did slay her in the Spirit, she would not hit her head, as she would already be on the floor. She lay down and after a few moments of prayer was baptized in the Holy Spirit.

LET THE CHILDREN COME

Jesus said, "Let the little children come to me, and do not hinder them, for the kingdom of heaven belongs to such as these" (Matthew 19:14). Letting children come to Jesus implies a kind invitation. For too many years, well-meaning Pentecostals have implored, pressured, scared, or even coerced children to come to altars to pray for the baptism in the Holy Spirit. It was almost as if receiving the gift took precedence over the practical application of the gift. Where is the fruit of the Spirit in an altar service that would press children to receive a gift for which they are not ready?

So, if you are a children's leader, I implore you to "let" the children come! Do not drag, threaten, trick, push, or pull children toward Jesus and the gifts He has for them. Do not tell scary stories that force them into a place of uncomfortable decision.

Mike introduced himself to me during the first altar service at a camp in Humble, Texas. As other children were praying, he approached me and said, "I don't want to pray." Rather than trying to force the goodness of God on this eleven-year-old boy, I replied, "Then just sit back and watch, Mike. If you have any questions, just find me and ask."

During the second and third nights of the camp, a similar exchange took place. Then Thursday night's service came. Mike came up to me with tears running down his face. He blurted out, "I'm ready now." Mike accepted Jesus as his Savior and was baptized in the Spirit at that altar. I am sure that if I had forced the issue earlier in the week, he would not have received.

Over the years, I have found that children want more of God. Scripture says, "Taste and see that the Lord is good" (Psalm 34:8). Our task as leaders is to present Jesus in such a way children will want to taste and see. Once they have had a taste of genuine prayer and praise they will develop a hunger that will last a lifetime. The baptism in the Holy Spirit is a wonderful gift that, once received, will give children the kind of hunger I am talking about.

My wife, Darlene, and I have four children. There have been times in each of their lives when we sat waiting at the dinner table as they tried a new food. Forcing this upon them rarely resulted in their wanting more of the mysterious substance. We learned that the presentation of a new food alongside other dishes they loved was a much better approach. In the same way, presenting a gift like the baptism in the Holy Spirit can be done in such a way as to excite the child's imagination and engage the child's desire for more of God. Forcing a child to "taste and see" this experience will reap little benefit in his or her life.

Be sure to present the baptism in the Holy Spirit and all that comes with it in a positive light. Illustrate the message in such a way as to water the garden of enthusiasm in their hearts. I've given you a couple of ideas, but so many more exist. It is important when presenting this lesson to illustrate it in a colorful, simple, child-friendly manner. Use objects, stories, and music that appeal to the child's senses and sensibility. Involve the children in the lesson. Do not hold an object yourself when you can employ a child to hold it for you. Do not just tell a story but bring children up front to act it out.

It is important you do not use scare tactics or spooky stories. Face it: some of the spiritual happenings surrounding adults receiving this gift can sound scary when explained to a child. The idea of suddenly speaking in an unknown tongue can be scary for a young one. Here is how I explain tongues. "God will do nothing scary to you. He does not come in and move your tongue uncontrollably. That would be scary. You praise Him in your own language and He will give you new words through your mind and spirit. You may hear or think a word or two. Say those words by faith as God gives you more and more of His Spirit. The words you say or language God gives you may not sound anything like me or others speaking around you. That's okay. God loves you so much that He wants to give you a special unique prayer language you can use when you don't know how to pray."

It is important to note that we want to encourage children to seek more of God. I like to compare it to Christmas. Certainly at Christmas you want to receive gifts from your grandparents. But the experience is so much richer when you get to do that with Grandpa or Grandma in the room to hug and love you. I encourage children not to worry about getting tongues, but instead to enjoy spending time with Jesus. "I love those who love me, and those who seek me find me" (Proverbs 8:17). "Come near to God and he will come near to you" (James 4:8).

Emphasis must not be placed on "getting tongues" but on being empowered by Jesus. Boys and girls need the power of the Holy Spirit in order to stand for God in these last days. To seek the gift without the Giver is to make the same mistake Simon did in Acts 8:18, when he offered money to receive the Holy Spirit.

LET THE CHILDREN PRAY

Children are full of faith and ready to pray at any time. In both camp and church settings, I have discovered that if we allow children to pray and give them time to do this, they will respond by storming the gates of heaven. One Sunday morning I opened the altars to children wishing to receive the baptism in the Holy Spirit. About a dozen children responded. When I invited friends to pray with them, more than thirty came down to help their peers. The prayer service went on until parents were coming in the back of the room. We invited these parents to join their children in prayer. Many did, and God moved in a marvelous way.

Stanley Grenz wrote, "Many Christians do not pray because they are not convinced that prayer works; they do not understand what prayer is, how prayer functions, or for what they should pray."[1] If this is true of the adult believers Stanley Grenz wrote about, it is also true of children. Our task as leaders of children is to help them experience God in real ways. We must teach on prayer, but not stop until children have experienced what we have taught about.

Children approach God with simple genuine faith. How many times has a child approached you asking that you pray for a plant, pet, or parent? The child who asks does not hesitate to believe you will pray and God will hear you. This same basic faith is utilized when a child prays to receive spiritual gifts from God. Once a child is allowed to come to Him, that child will receive from Him.

Don Crawford wrote, "We call not on a father who is preoccupied with his career and has little time for his children. We call not on a father who may find someone else he loves more and so forsake us. Nor does the father on whom we call simply cater to our whims while we manipulate him."[2] God is always available to listen to and answer the prayers of children.

I had a group of Royal Rangers commanders who wanted to host a Holy Spirit night in their third-grade group. They laid out the plan for the evening and invited me to come pray for children at about 7:30 that evening. They taught and readied the boys and in my absence began to pray. I arrived in the room at about 7:45 to the sound of two dozen third-grade boys on their faces before God, praying their hardest. Several boys had received the Holy Spirit prior to my arrival. These boys were praying for and encouraging friends to receive this gift.

Boys and girls will pray if we will allow it. They will wait before God if we give them time to do so. They will receive the good gifts of God if we encourage them.

LET THE CHILDREN ENJOY

Finally, I want to address the concept of letting children enjoy the presence of God. Seeking the baptism in the Holy Spirit should not be painful, distressing, or scary for any child. Yet I have talked with children and adults who sought this gift as a child who have had tragic experiences at altars.

One man told me that every evangelist who came through his church shook him and yelled at him and tried to somehow force the gift into him. This man didn't receive the Holy Spirit until he was in his late twenties. This brings to mind the fact that if you are a children's leader, you are not the baptizer. Let God be God and baptize children when they are ready and when the time is right. There is nothing you can do to force this experience to happen. You cannot yell loudly enough or speak a magic formula to cause this to happen in children's lives. Let Jesus gently draw children in.

I have met many children who, when leaving the altar without having received, felt guilty or insignificant. One girl cried that if she didn't go home from camp with the gift of tongues her mom would be upset. What happened to trusting God? How can we as leaders feel justified in presenting a wonderful gift like the baptism in the Holy Spirit in such a way that those who do not receive feel like second-class believers?

I exhort you to encourage every child who prays for this gift. I talk to children at the conclusion of or following an altar service. I congratulate all who have prayed. I encourage those who have received to use that prayer language every chance they get. I encourage those who have not yet received to continue believing. They have asked God to fill them to overflowing with His Spirit. He is going to do this in their lives. I tell them, "Walk away from this altar expecting that at any time the overflowing will happen and you will speak in another tongue."

One group of about a dozen ten- and eleven-year-old girls came excitedly to me after an altar service in a hotel meeting room. By their own testimony, all had prayed for most of an hour. None had received. They chose to go back to their rooms believing God would baptize them at any minute. When they all entered the elevator with their counselor, one girl hit the button for their floor. When her finger touched that button, everyone on that elevator was baptized in the Spirit.

A nine-year-old boy shared with me at breakfast one day that he was walking to the restroom in the middle of the night. As he walked, he was singing a worship song. Soon the words he was singing were not English.

A group of girls in Missouri held hands and prayed before starting a volleyball game one afternoon at camp. As they prayed for the game, the Holy Spirit came upon them. Both teams were simultaneously baptized in the Spirit right there by the volleyball net. They were so blessed they didn't get around to playing.

I could go on and on with more testimonies. I think you get my point. When we as leaders of children make this experience all about Jesus, kids will receive and will have a great time doing so. Relax and let God work. In camp and crusade settings, there is a certain amount of pressure placed on leaders and preachers to produce results. Set that pressure aside in favor of allowing children to enjoy being in the presence of God.

One night at a camp in Minnesota, ten-year-old Jon was gloriously filled with the Spirit. He sang and prayed in his prayer language. He danced and jumped and ran through the altar service for over a half an hour. All of that time Jon's eyes were closed and tears of joy were running off of his cheeks—he was enjoying the presence of God. I know some leaders would have stopped him. I'm glad we didn't. Jon had a unique experience I have never witnessed before or since.

Part of assisting children in enjoying the baptism in the Holy Spirit involves instructing them concerning all of the extra manifestations that can occur when a person receives this gift of God. A child may cry one time while praying and laugh another. He or she may feel nothing while speaking in tongues or they may feel deep emotions. Boys and girls need to hear this is normal.

Some have been "slain in the Spirit" while praying. Right next to them others are having just as valid a prayer experience without the same response. I have witnessed children give prophetic utterances, words of knowledge, and tongues and interpretation at altars. It is exciting to be used of God! I encourage children to seek to be used, and I tell them God will give them just the right gift at just the right time.

CONCLUSION

Here are some bullet points to remember that will help you to better serve children when addressing the subject of the baptism in the Holy Spirit.

Stay away from extremes.
Teach using simple terms.
Encourage children to pray.
Ask God for direction.
Do not ignore this subject.
You can be used of God.

Stay away from extremes

Extreme approaches to spiritual happenings can be really scary to younger children. Try not to overemphasize personal preferences over scriptural imperatives. If the Bible isn't specific concerning a method or manifestation, then seek God as to how He wants the service to progress.

Teach using simple terms

I am not proposing you dumb down this gift or any presentation of it. Be a wise teacher and make certain you are using child-friendly language and illustrations.

Encourage children to pray

I remind you that boys and girls love to pray. With a little encouragement, extending time available, and a nice altar area, kids can and will pray until the parents drag them away. Prayer should be encouraged as an everyday habit.

Ask God for direction

Seek God whenever you plan to present this subject. I try not to hang my current presentation on success in the past. I seek God anew each time I present this and I ask for His anointing to be fresh.

Do not ignore this subject

You may be afraid of doing something wrong when teaching about the Holy Spirit to children. Do not let that stop you. If you sincerely seek God's direction and have right motives in presenting this, I believe God will come through for you. His desire is for boys and girls everywhere to receive all He has for them.

You can be used of God

When it comes to helping children receive the baptism in the Holy Spirit, God does not show favoritism. You may be uneducated or highly educated, rich or poor, a pastor or a parishioner. I implore you to set aside any inadequacies you may feel and trust God. He is the Baptizer. God has always been blessing people. He will continue to do so. You can be God's instrument of blessing in the lives of the children you serve. Let God bless the children through you as you present the baptism in the Holy Spirit to His beloved little ones.

1. Stanley Grenz, *Prayer: The Cry For The Kingdom* (Peabody, MA: Hendrickson, 1988), 47.
2. Dan Crawford, *The Prayer Shaped Disciple* (Peabody, MA: Hendrickson, 1999), 5.

CHAPTER ELEVEN

COMMUNICATING THE CHARACTER OF THE HOLY SPIRIT TO KIDS

By Jim Gerhold

When we talk to kids, it's important to have good, solid communication on who the Holy Spirit is. Our approach should be short and simple—simplistic in our methodology and simplistic in our concepts so that it's easy to understand and grasp. We should stay away from terminology that would raise any kind of question marks. If we use terms and illustrations that kids can easily grasp, it will be easier for us to lead them.

It's important that kids understand the Holy Spirit is the Spirit of God. The Trinity can be difficult to explain, even to adults. Matthew 28:19 commands us to "go and make disciples of all nations, baptizing them in the name of the Father and of the Son and of the Holy Spirit." The three Persons in the Godhead work together as one for the benefit of all. But the main truth is that the Holy Spirit is the Spirit of God.

The Holy Spirit is part of our Christian living; He's part of our continuing growth. He's an overcoming power, a faith builder, He's our guide, our "point person"—in the military this means "the lead person," or "the person watching out for danger." He's a teacher and tutor. He's a comforter. He's the One who brings reassurance and calmness to our life.

These things need to be communicated well to our kids, and always in simple ways they can understand.

EXPLAINING THE BAPTISM IN THE HOLY SPIRIT TO KIDS

To illustrate the promise of the baptism in the Spirit, I like to write a check, scan it, and print it out much larger. I talk about how a check is made out to a specific person but has no value unless it's cashed. In Luke 24:49, Jesus promised that the Holy Spirit will be given as promised, and He told the disciples to go and stay in the city of Jerusalem until the Holy Spirit filled them with power. So it is a promise. I like to define the word "promise" as a guarantee, pledge, or covenant. "I've given you my word and this is what I'm going to do."

The Baptism is a gift, so I define the gift. God wants the very best for us, so He's given us the gift of the Holy Spirit to enhance our spiritual lives.

Then, just for fun, I present the Top 10 facts of God's gift-giving process:

10. God loves to give gifts.
9. Because God cares, He gives the best, kind of like Hallmark.
8. God wants everything in our lives to be better, so He gives us things that will enhance our lives.
7. All gifts given by God are heavenly, wonderful things we'll love and enjoy.
6. God does not give bogus gifts, only things that are useful, practical, and fun.
5. We need God's gifts in our lives.
4. A gift from God is free.
3. A gift from God is supposed to be used every day of our lives.
2. Once God gives a gift, He's not going to take it back.
1. God gives us all these gifts because He loves us and really cares for us and He wants the very best for us.

AVOIDING INEFFECTIVE TECHNIQUES

We can hinder kids by some of the things we do. We can bring confusion and division and give children a wrong concept of what God really wants. The Holy Spirit is willing to fill kids; we are there merely to be His assistants and to guide a child through any confusion or fears he or she may have. Therefore, we have to be careful of what we do and say because we can negatively influence children for the rest of their lives.

We need to be careful not to do anything that will embarrass a child or make him or her feel awkward. When we pray with kids around the altars, we take on a heavy responsibility. If children are not filled with the Holy Spirit and have a bitter or bad experience, they may not come back to the altar the next time. And many times these things can carry over to adulthood. Some adults who are not Spirit-filled today had negative or manipulative childhood experiences and still deal with that emotional baggage.

We can relieve any kind of fears or tensions children have by just talking to them calmly and in an easy, soft voice. Answer any questions to the best of your ability. I always remind someone who has a fear of the Baptism that the Holy Spirit is a gentleman. He's not going to make you do something that's uncomfortable, He's not going to come in and embarrass you. He's here to help you grow in the Lord.

I want kids to have fond memories of what God has done around the altars. When we come home from a kids' camp, I want them to say, "Oh, God did such a neat thing. I was slain in the Spirit, and for an hour I was lost in the presence of God," or "I remember how He filled me, and it was so wonderful," or "He healed me." I want kids to come back with great memories of the altars at camps. And I want kids on Sunday morning to know that I'm not going to do anything that's going to make them feel awkward and they're not going to have to do anything crazy or outlandish. I want them to have a good, healthy understanding and experience.

As pastors and leaders, we are the gateway. Children will either accept or reject the Baptism based largely on what we communicate, so we have to be very careful. Treat each child as an individual; pray for him or her and speak with great sensitivity.

CORRECTING MISCONCEPTIONS ABOUT THE HOLY SPIRIT

A lot of kids have misconceptions about the Holy Spirit. For example, a young man in a wheelchair gave his heart to God at camp. The next night he just sat in the back during the altar time.

I asked him, "Would you like to have more from God and be filled with the Spirit?"

He said, "God's not going to fill me, because I'm handicapped. I have a defect."

He had drawn a very wrong conclusion. His handicap had caused him to be rejected by others. So I spent about twenty minutes with him, explaining that his handicap is only a physical thing.

"You can be filled with the Holy Spirit easily," I assured him. "A wheelchair doesn't affect that."

So I wheeled him to the altar, and some counselors gathered around him and prayed. About an hour later he received the Holy Spirit.

Sometimes we can forget those who haven't responded. It can be tragic not to be sensitive to the Holy Spirit. We need to reassure kids that God never rejects anyone; there is no favoritism with Him. God loves us all the same.

Another misconception is that the Baptism is the final stop and that kids have "arrived" spiritually when they speak in tongues. Our spiritual life is supposed to continue to grow, and the Holy Spirit helps us to do that. Once we're filled, it's another step, another level, another dimension that is intended to continue developing.

A third misconception arises when kids don't want to be filled with the Holy Spirit because they've heard something negative or they were in a church where they've had some teaching against the Holy Spirit. You have to patiently open the Scriptures and share with them that the Holy Spirit is part of the package of living for God. God has a plan for their lives, and the Holy Spirit is part of that plan. The Baptism is the next step.

PRACTICAL TIPS FOR PRODUCTIVE ALTAR TIME

As leaders, our attitude is probably 90 percent of the battle when it comes to leading kids into the Baptism. Because we are agents who can help people to the next level, we need to create an expectation of what God can do in their lives. We must be positive role models for them. If they see something positive and exciting in us, then that creates a hunger and desire for more of God. But if they see a nonchalant attitude in our approach, then why should they want to ever receive the Holy Spirit?

If the child is apprehensive, I will pray in front of that child in English and then I'll also begin to pray in the Spirit. This helps to break the ice so children can see that praying in the Spirit is part of my prayer life. I'll gently place my hand on their shoulder, being careful not to push too hard or invade their space or make them feel awkward. I'll give the child some simple direction when they need it—some do, some don't.

If children are very distracted, it doesn't mean they won't receive. I'll approach them and say, "Hey, pray with me for a minute." Sometimes I'll ask, "Do you really want the Holy Spirit tonight?" And if they say yes, I'll continue, "Okay, let's refocus. You're being distracted by some of your buddies, or maybe you're just watching what is going on around you—so let's refocus." Sometimes I'll encourage them to close their eyes and begin to worship God. This is common with kids: they were worshipping a few moments ago, and then they began to look around and their thoughts turned to the things around them. So I try to refocus them on worshipping and seeking.

Some kids respond to an altar call and are immediately filled with the Spirit. Other kids seem like they're struggling or frustrated. When a kid is struggling, I'll ask questions that are no-brainers to reinforce the positive.

"You know God really loves you, don't you?"
"Yes."
"You know God wants to give you the very best, right?"
"Right."
"You know the Holy Spirit is here tonight, right?"
"Yes."
"Okay. Now, do you have any fears or concerns?"

I try to find out what the apprehension is. Kids may give you one of the classic answers like, "I'm not good enough," or "I don't know if I'm really ready for it." Work them through whatever the issue may be. "So, how do you know that you're not ready for it?" I try to address the specific fear or apprehension that is causing them not to receive the Holy Spirit.

INSTRUCTING KIDS IN RECEIVING THE BAPTISM

Once you educate kids, it's time to put into practice what's been learned. After I've given kids all this information in terms that allow them to comprehend what the Baptism is all about, it's time for them to receive. When it comes to actually receiving, it's not my job to fill them; that's God's job. It is my job to help facilitate and encourage their baptism in the Spirit without gimmicks or manipulation.

The main instruction is to tell kids to focus on the Lord. "Start putting your mind on God. If you want to close your eyes and forget what's around you, then do that. Think of something God has done for you and thank Him for it."

As kids begin to thank the Lord for what He's done in their lives, they are opening the door to receive from God. I often model that for them as I begin to thank God for things. I'll tell the children, "Just keep speaking out praise and worship, using your mouth and your tongue." Nine times out of ten, they'll be filled with the Spirit right then. Sometimes it is just that easy because kids are so open.

Kids who are more open to the work of the Spirit can

help other kids. A couple of years ago in a Royal Rangers awards ceremony, two or three boys came forward to pray for the Baptism. One boy received within seconds. The boy next to him was struggling. After a few minutes of working with him, I realized I wasn't getting through to him. That's when I looked over at the first boy who was still speaking in tongues and praising God. So I had the two face each other and asked the first boy to pray for the second. I just stepped back. Within minutes, the second child just exploded in praise to God, and before long he was speaking in tongues.

I try to encourage children to use their voice and lips and begin to speak out loud in praise to God. That way, when the Holy Spirit comes on them it's just one more step. All of a sudden, they're going from English to a heavenly language.

FOUR SIMPLE OBJECT LESSONS

It's a tried-and-true principle in ministry—familiar, simple illustrations can illuminate the unfamiliar. Jesus did this with His parables to point people toward the kingdom of God. You can use simple object lessons to point children to the wonderful work of the Holy Spirit in their lives. Here are a few suggestions.

The first example is an electrical plug. Hold up a small lamp and tell the kids, "This reminds me of the power we have in God. The Holy Spirit is a great source of power. But if we never plug this lamp into the wall, if we never put this plug into the outlet, we'll never get the power. We can have the power to overcome temptations and be a strong witness in a lost world, but we have to get plugged in with the Holy Spirit. Just as this fixture will never do anything unless we plug it into the power supply, our lives will never be what they could be until we plug into God's power."

Another object lesson deals with building up our faith to receive the Holy Spirit. I'll use a three or five pound weight and have a kid dress up in a sweat suit. He'll pump iron while I talk about the importance of physical strength and how we should be building our muscles. In the same way we build our physical bodies, we need to develop our spiritual lives. We need to be reading the Word and praying in the Spirit to build our spiritual muscles. Praying in the Spirit is a spiritual force the devil has a hard time competing against, because we can overcome temptations and obstacles through the Holy Spirit.

Another object lesson focuses on the Holy Spirit being a guide to us. I'll come out wearing a tourist hat and holding a road map, acting like I'm lost. I'll say, "Aw, man, I'm trying to get to New York, but I can't get there." And I hold up my map, and say, "Oh, I know why; I took the wrong route." I'll talk about how the Holy Spirit is our guide in our walk with God and how He gives us direction and helps us with our decisions. "I made a wrong decision, and I ended up in Los Angeles. Now how do I get back to New York? I get back to the road map!" The Holy Spirit does that. He is like our sense of right or wrong, our conscience. And when we've read the Scriptures, He will bring the truth back to our memory. That's part of His promise. That's part of who He is.

For a fourth object lesson, I talk about a gift-wrapped package. Special gifts express to me that I'm loved. God loves us, so He has many, many gifts to give us. I'll have several gifts for the kids to see and I'll open one each session. I'll say, "You know what? I could give all of these out right now, but I'm going to give another one out next time." That brings the expectation up. One of the packages will represent the baptism in the Holy Spirit.

In the end, whether I'm explaining the Baptism in simple terms and with simple illustrations, or gently praying with a child to receive the Baptism, it really comes down to how full of the Spirit I am. As I remain Pentecostal in practice and lifestyle, I can count on the Holy Spirit using me to point the youngest followers of Christ to Him and His many gifts.

CHAPTER TWELVE

COMMUNICATING THE BAPTISM IN THE HOLY SPIRIT TO STUDENTS

By Allen Griffin

When communicating the baptism in the Holy Spirit with young people, you have to realize that they are looking for a personal connection. "How is this going to affect *me*?" Secondly, you must realize that students are focused on the moment. How the Baptism affected people in the past is important, but not as important as what the Baptism is going to do today. "What is this going to do for me *now*?"

We can share the truth of the Holy Spirit without making them totally afraid of God. They need to know He is not going to send a "lightning bolt" from heaven, or do something they've seen on TV that might not be a great example of receiving the Baptism. We can draw students to this experience and remind them this is a dynamic experience, a receiving of the power of God. It's an awakening that will bring a life change. It's tapping into the power of God that brings transformation—and I believe young people are interested in that power.

PROCLAIMING THE BAPTISM IN THE HOLY SPIRIT

Life is basically about power. Young people want power. That's why the Internet has come into their lives—it gives them power.

The ability to control not only the music they listen to but how they listen to it gives them power. The earlier generation would listen to a CD all the way through. This generation logs on to the Internet and downloads one song they like off of an album. They want power—the ability to make a choice and to do something with that choice.

When we present the Holy Spirit to them, we're giving them the choice to receive God's anointing, God's power, and then the ability to function with that power. In order to explain this better, I often use the example of electricity—the alternating current in the walls of our homes, offices, and schools. Before electricity, people used oil lamps because there were no light bulbs. There were no modern heaters, so they used fireplaces. Air conditioning wasn't created until 1906, so they used hand fans. Life is better today in every aspect because of electric power. The Holy Spirit's role is to make mankind better, taking an average young person and giving him or her power.

In the Old Testament, the power would come upon people and they would do great things. Now, that power is for everyone and it stays with us. The Holy Spirit lives with us and communes with us. His power allows us to do the work of the great men and women of old. *Everyone* can operate in the power of the Spirit and do great things for the kingdom of God.

The number one fear in the world is not death. The number one fear in the world is not pain. The number one fear in the world is public speaking. The number one fear in the world is influenced, affected, and changed by God; the power of the Holy Spirit has come to make us bold. He gives us the ability to stand with courage, faith, and strength to do what God has called us to do. This gift affects that fear.

MINISTERING THE BAPTISM IN THE HOLY SPIRIT

When I was sixteen, I received the Holy Spirit. When I was seventeen, I believed that for some reason I was creative enough to create this language, so for two and a half years I faked the baptism in the Holy Spirit. It wasn't until I was almost twenty years old that the Holy Spirit finally broke through and revealed to me that He had given me the Baptism. I learned that I couldn't have done it. I couldn't make it up. I'm not that creative and I'm certainly not that smart! Then I finally believed.

One thing I've found that helps explain the Baptism to young people is to share the story about how God filled you with the Holy Spirit. Were you afraid? Were you doubtful?

Share your experience transparently with students. Some will struggle with the same issues you struggled with and you will open up their minds and they'll be more ready to receive.

At this point I believe the approach needs to be instructional. I say this very specifically as an evangelist: the emotional and exciting part should be in the message, not in the method. We don't want to fill them with emotion when they're about to receive this gift. Most students struggle to receive the baptism in the Holy Spirit because they don't have enough information, not because they don't have enough emotion. Give clear instruction on exactly how they can receive.

These students want all the information they can get. Try to be linear in your presentation, going from where you are now to where you want to be. Here's an example of how to explain the preparation for receiving to students:

"First, you're going to come forward. Second, I'm going to ask you to raise your hands. It's just a physical exercise of posturing yourself before God, of humility, of reception. Then, I'm going to come down, and I'm going to lay my hand on your head, or leaders are going to lay their hands on your head. No lightning bolts are going to come from heaven, but we're going to ask God for His Holy Spirit. We have examples in the Bible that through the laying on of hands this gift was given, so we want to pray that way."

Tell them everything you're going to do so when they come forward and begin to pray they aren't surprised. They need to know what's going on. Pray for them corporately first, before praying for individuals. Many students are ready to receive during praise and worship, even before you pray for them individually.

You should also be very aware of young people who need personal time with the Lord or personal attention in prayer. Don't just roam around in a spiritual haze. Go to each student individually. Lay hands on him or her. Pay attention to whom you're praying with.

If the student is not praying at that moment, look him or her in the eye and offer some basic guidance. Here is a sample conversation:

"Hey, what's your name?"

"My name is Barbara."

"All right, Barbara. My name is Allen."

This breaks the ice, especially if the student is nervous.

"Okay, Barbara. I'm going to pray for you right now, that you'll receive the baptism in the Holy Spirit. Are you ready to receive it? Do you have any questions?"

Take your time; don't be in a hurry. When she says, "Yes, I'm ready; I don't really have any questions," then continue.

"Okay, Barbara. In a moment, I want you to raise your hands, and I'm going to pray. What I want you to do is to listen to God. If you want to worship and listen, that's fine. If you want to pray and listen, then go ahead and pray and listen. The Lord's going to speak to you. The Holy Spirit will give you words to speak and you need to speak them. I don't know what kind of language it's going to be, Barbara, but whatever you hear from God, speak it, and don't stop. Are you ready? Okay. All right, raise your hands."

Many times, students will say to you, "I can't hear God. What does He sound like? How does God speak?"

The best way I have found to explain it is:

"When the Spirit of God speaks to me personally, it's like I can feel it and hear it at the same time. It's almost like your dad is talking to you, and you put your head on his chest when he's talking. You can hear what he's saying and feel what he's saying. It's very similar to that.

"God speaks to us, and He's able to work through all of our senses, not just one. Sometimes you'll feel an urgency of the Spirit. I believe you're going to hear from God. Whether or not your emotions are involved doesn't matter, but you will hear from God.

"He speaks to you as if you were going to say something, and a thought comes to your mind of what you're going to say. You're probably not going to hear God announce, 'Attention, this is God, and I've got something to say.' What you're going to receive is a God-inspired thought—a good thought—that you're able to speak because you received it from God directly."

I have seen so many students receive the Baptism this way. They're ready and prepared, they've been instructed—so they're not surprised. Through teaching, instruction, and agreeing in prayer, something is triggered by faith and they receive from God.

CHALLENGES TO THE BAPTISM IN THE HOLY SPIRIT

What happens if no one in your group is filled? I was a youth pastor for years in Miami, and there was a night where I decided it was time to lead our students into the baptism in the Holy Spirit. I preached the best I could, then called students to the altar and had them raise their hands as I started to pray over them. Out of all of my students, not one was filled with the Holy Spirit. There were between 150 and 200 students and leaders in the room. How do you deal with a service where nobody gets filled?

When no one is filled, don't blame it on your group by saying, "They're not spiritual." You need to look at the makeup of your group and discover what their learning and communication styles are, along with what stage of faith they are in. Church kids who have been disappointed many times by speakers, or disappointed many times at altars require extra sensitivity. When we look at the experiences of our students, we need to make sure we fill the need in their life. Ask them questions about what they know about the Spirit. Teach by using what you know about them; it may help overcome some of the challenges.

Within six months, I had dealt with my youth group's issues and I had fixed my psyche from all the abuse I'd given myself for what I considered a failure—which really was just a lack of training. My students began to be filled, and I had what many would consider a very spiritual, Holy Spirit-filled youth ministry. Please understand, if they don't want to receive, they won't receive, no matter how hard you pray, no matter how hard you work.

Another challenge is students who have wired their mouth shut mentally. There are some students who won't speak out when you pray for them; they won't even open their mouths. Sometimes they're waiting for God to move their mouth for them. Sometimes they're just quiet people by nature. Again, you need to look at what you know about the student. If you know that they're more quiet, then just encourage them that the Spirit's not going to force them. The Spirit will speak into their life, and they have to choose to respond.

If students refuse to open their mouth and speak, sometimes I'll even say, "Hey, you know what? You don't have to even speak what you hear loud enough for me to hear, but you need to speak it loud enough so that you know you're saying it." Don't force them to raise their voices, or to do exactly what you do.

How long should students wait at the altar? As long as they possibly can! That means as long as students want to wait and as long as parents are willing to wait. If you feel some students really need to leave, have your leaders go to them individually and ask if they feel like they need to go. If they say yes, then have a leader walk them out and then come back in. If people are still pursuing the Baptism, don't make a general dismissal. Let students pursue God as long as they want.

One of the greatest concerns I've had in ministry is people who have twenty minutes of altar time and two hours of games. If we're going to have an encounter with God, we must be willing to sacrifice some time. Time with God is love, and we must give God as much of our love as we can. That's our time. It's the most valuable commodity we have. We should tarry as long as students want to, as long as they'll wait, as long as they can.

Another challenge is often the different types of responses that may take place. Remember that a young person's personality is part of the process of receiving the baptism in the Holy Spirit. I love this about God: He created the personality of every person who is receiving. And if God created our personalities, God is not going to give us the power of the Holy Spirit to remove our own personality but to enhance it. If a student is a quieter person, more of a solitary type, God is not going to turn him or her into a raving, roving, running, jumping, crazy person. If a student is more outgoing and receives the baptism in the Holy Spirit, he or she is probably not going to become a quiet person. Students keep their own personality, but now with the power of the Holy Spirit.

Also, don't be a distraction. You're a coach. Encourage them, but do not force them to do anything outside of their character. Pray that they hear from God. If they dance, sway, rock, shake, or cry, that's fine. But don't instigate any action, or it will be a distraction. There are times when I will hold back my personality and my enthusiasm so I can keep myself from distracting the person who's pursuing the presence of God.

Many leaders want students to look a certain way. Don't think that if your group is not responding the way you're used to that they're not filled with the Spirit. Perhaps you can say, "You know what? However you respond is great, as long as you respond." Encourage them that whatever they say, whatever they've heard from God and responded to is okay, and that you're excited for them.

So, what is life like *after* the power of the Holy Spirit? How will it affect young people today?

LIVING THE BAPTISM IN THE HOLY SPIRIT

After students have received the baptism in the Holy Spirit, many times we stop and say, "Man, you received the baptism in the Holy Spirit. That's great, you're done." But we shouldn't want to stop there. God doesn't want believers to stop there either. He wants us to continue to be filled.

We need to let the Holy Spirit do what the Holy Spirit does through us as leaders, and let the students see it. Don't hesitate to pray for miracles as a leader. Pray and believe that powerful things are going to happen, then step out and allow the Holy Spirit to flow through you in the service. Pray for the word of knowledge to flow;

pray for prophecy to flow in the lives of young people.

We don't want to send our young people out to fail. We don't want them to stumble through the gifts of the Spirit. We want to challenge them to operate in spiritual gifts in our services so that when the time comes and they're in a secular scenario, they can look at someone and say, "This is what God has shared with me for you." They can know they heard from God because the gifts of the Spirit are practiced in their youth service.

After I received the Baptism, I began using it in witnessing. As I'd go out and witness, God would begin to speak to me and reveal things to me I couldn't have known apart from the Spirit.

Within two weeks after I had received the baptism in the Holy Spirit, my pastor and I, along with several other young men, went to a huge park in Detroit. My pastor said to us, "Okay, we're going to witness. We're three hours away from home; you don't know any of these people here. I want to start teaching you here, and then we're going to go home and talk to the people we actually know."

So we started walking around the park and praying, and I was using my new prayer language. My youth pastor walked up to me, grabbed me by the arm, and said, "Okay; you're going to walk with me across this park, and I'm going to introduce us to the first people that we see. Then I want you to tell them whatever the Holy Spirit wants you to tell them. I believe God's going to tell you their names; God's going to tell you information about them they never told you, and then you're going to be able to lead them to God. I want you to ask Him to do that."

As we walked across the park, I thought, *Okay, God, You're going to have to tell me something about these people that I don't know, because there is no way that I can know it on my own.*

Two young men were walking towards us; one was as big as a football player and the other was a slim guy. As we got closer, it got a little bit uncomfortable! I continued speaking in my new language—I was speaking it faster and faster as we got closer. Finally, my youth pastor looked at the two young men and said, "My name is Jeff, and this is my friend Allen. And Allen has something he wants you to know."

Right when he said that, the Holy Spirit began to speak to me. When I opened my mouth, I couldn't believe what I was saying! There was such courage in me coming from the Spirit. I wasn't afraid; I was at peace. I looked at them and said, "Your name is Mike, and your name is Steve, and you're walking across this park because you just ordered a pizza, and you're heading over to a pizza place around the corner, and God sent me here from Grand Rapids to tell you that Jesus loves you."

Well, both of those young men looked at me like I was crazy. I thought maybe I was wrong, and so I started to lower my head. The big dude, whose name was Mike, spoke up first. He looked at me and said, "Where are you from? How do you know our names?"

I looked up at him, and the courage of God filled me, and I said, "I'm not even from here." I pulled out my wallet and showed them I was from a different school district and from a different city. It took a long time to explain that it was God that shared this information with me, but it didn't take long for them to believe in the God we serve and to accept Jesus Christ right there in that park.

If we allow the Spirit to use us, there's nothing that will be impossible. Miracles and signs and wonders "will accompany those who believe" (Mark 16:17). Too many times we want to stop at the baptism in the Holy Spirit.

Why not pray for miracles? Have students pray for each other. When God begins to perform miracles, students will believe and understand that they can take part in the miraculous. When the Spirit of God comes upon a believer, you have the power to do miracles. The Spirit gives life, and we need to operate in that new life. Young people will take that everywhere they go.

May all of us allow the Spirit to use this generation to do greater things than we ever imagined we could do.

Chapter Thirteen

Preparing a Leadership Team

By Nate Ruch

No generation is more primed for a Pentecostal relationship with God through the baptism in the Holy Spirit than the millennial generation. Our students in elementary, middle, and high school have grown up in a culture that values participation as a prerequisite to belief. Kids build relationships through text messaging, networked video gaming, personal networking pages, cell phones, and TV shows that allow viewers to vote and determine which contestant makes it to the next round. If we could help today's young generation engage in the explosive promise of the Holy Spirit baptism, this group is primed to live it out in ways previous generations never dreamed of.

In my youth homiletics course at North Central University, every student must preach a message on the baptism in the Holy Spirit. Each semester I see students with scared looks on their faces as we begin. I lead a discussion with these future youth pastors and ask their reasons for being afraid.

The many different explanations offered typically point back to a couple of common sources. The first is a lack of model pastors preaching and leading their church in Spirit baptism—other than possibly once a year. Future pastors who have not heard model pastors preach on Spirit baptism are reluctant to preach about it themselves.

The second source of fear is a frustration from negative personal experiences. As a result of their frustration, many pastors today have left the responsibility of leading students in the Baptism to evangelists, rather than cultivate this wonderful opportunity within their own ministry.

Pastoral and volunteer leadership teams within youth ministries must fill the gap between students in this generation and God's promise of spiritual empowerment through the baptism in the Holy Spirit. Every leader must be considered a conduit who plays a decisive role in the activation of this promise. The elements that follow are critical for leaders in order to unleash a spiritually empowered generation.

PASTORAL LEADERSHIP

It may seem obvious, but nonetheless it's true—kids figure out what is important spiritually by what is emphasized in their church. The pastor impacts students through the influence of the leadership team, by preaching, and by implementing ministry strategies that teach kids to believe. If kids aren't participating in the promise of the Baptism, the question is why not? If you believe that the Baptism is an important part of your own spirituality, it is just as needed by the students you lead. So how do you help them?

The totality of ministry strategy needs to be considered when thinking about students being empowered through the Baptism. Small groups, Sunday School, services, activities, curriculum, devotionals, discipleship programs, worship, missions trips—literally every point of contact with students is a potential consideration for the strategy of releasing kids to be filled with the Spirit. Many traditional Pentecostal church strategies only address Spirit baptism within the context of a service. The service is a wonderful context in which young people can receive, but it is not the only setting.

Small groups are a worthy avenue in which to explore the baptism in the Holy Spirit and cultivate Pentecostal ministry.

Instructions in the New Testament address churches that closely resemble small groups both in size and in composition. Small groups are relational environments where people can seek the Baptism. A small group setting can also be an environment more conducive for newly Spirit-baptized students to step out and function in spiritual gifts. Unfortunately, this valuable ministry setting is often not used in this way. Volunteer leader training is essential for this to occur and will be covered later.

PREACHING/PRESENTING THE BAPTISM IN THE HOLY SPIRIT

I think the easiest part of leading students in the Baptism is preaching about it—if you do. Telling students that God has more opportunities for blessing available can be exhilarating when done in faith, much like preaching on salvation. The danger here is you could be tempted to preach your feelings. As a mentor of mine says, "Don't just preach your feelings, preach the Word!" The truth is that you only have the responsibility to provide the wood on the altar. God sets it on fire.

There are a few practical items to consider when presenting Spirit baptism in your preaching:

Preach on it more than once a year

One common complaint of my youth homiletics students is that the presentation and altar call at a youth camp is often emotion-driven and full of pressure. Well, if you were a kid and you knew there was only one night a year you would have a chance to receive the Baptism, you would be emotional too! Kids wouldn't have to experience this if there was a more regular opportunity to experience God's promise of the Baptism under the preaching of their pastor in their church.

Preaching a sermon series on the subject can allow the pastor to explore the biblical foundations, expose barriers, and build faith in the group. A series also places the Baptism at least on the level with the annual dating series in February or the evangelism emphasis leading up to the big community outreach. At the minimum, regularly addressing how to live a Spirit-filled life in the context of other sermon topics can help students—and all believers—appropriate the Baptism as a part of their daily life and not just once a year on Pentecost Sunday.

Use different vocabulary

It is amazing to me how words can mean different things to different people. Terms such as "Pentecost," "tongues," "slain in the Spirit" and "baptized in the Holy Spirit" all can evoke a different response based on an individual's experience in the religious world. Insiders may understand the meaning of these terms, but people who come from a different church or do not have any religious affiliation may be confused or uncomfortable.

Perhaps a new vocabulary that makes sense to the group each pastor works with is the best option. I use different words to describe what some would call obvious Pentecostal terms. Instead of "tongues" I use the term "spiritual language." When encouraging students to operate in the prophetic gift, I use the term "God-inspired words." The point is, the terms we use need to invite the people God has called us to serve into a deeper walk with the Spirit.

Use real-world illustrations

In our current church culture, much of the power promised by Jesus to be witnesses is only realized within the context of a church service. This should not be. Without guidance, kids could begin to think the baptism in the Holy Spirit is exercised by sharing a gift of the Spirit (1 Corinthians 12 and 13) with other believers who are in a service. Preaching must serve to help young Christians visualize utilizing the Baptism outside the church.

This can be accomplished by using common visual aids and stories. For example, I wanted to show students at a camp that a relationship with the Holy Spirit doesn't mean you suddenly are out of range for temptation. You still have to say no to sin. I told a story about my oldest son who really wanted to cut our grass by using the family lawn mower. One day, I looked in the backyard and David was pushing the low bar on the machine and my wife had her arms around him on the high bar, and they mowed the lawn together. David rushed into the house saying, "I mowed the lawn!" It was true, he did mow the lawn, but it was my wife who extended her arms around our son and helped him push over the hills he couldn't do on his own. I related this story to the common disciplines of life we are called to live. When we don't have what it takes, the Holy Spirit helps us "finish the lawn." As I told that story, I had a lawn mower on the platform in front of me. I listed common real-life difficulties the Holy Spirit promises to help us push through.

Another illustration involves our spiritual language, or tongues. Some kids struggle with how to implement this special gift into their everyday life. I like to use the illustration of getting lost in a forest. I don't know where I am and I'm scared. I can pull out a handheld GPS that bounces a signal off a satellite that tells me where I am and gives me the courage to move on. Similarly, when I'm in a public situation and don't feel God's presence, I might feel lost in terms of what to do next. I can speak in my spiritual language and know God is with me. When I know God is with me, I have more courage to step out and operate in other gifts. I can be in public school, pray, and then speak a prophetic (God-inspired) word to someone, knowing God is truly with me.

I think students are searching for ways to bridge all of their Christian life to their world from their experiences in church services. The more illustrations we give them of how this can happen, the more likely they will live in the Word when they go to school the next day.

Plan for a response time

Surprisingly, many preachers spend the majority of their time preparing their message and decide to wing it during the altar call. I'm a firm believer in every part of the altar call being considered beforehand. How will you make your appeal? Whom are you asking to respond? Where do you want them to move? What do they do when they are there? Do you want music? What songs? What do you want the audience members who didn't respond to do? All these questions should be answered ahead of time.

My friend, Wayne Northup, is a youth evangelist who has led thousands of teenagers to receive the Baptism and has developed a specific process through which he takes everyone who responds to an altar call. None of this process is a formula, just a list of key things to cover in order to help students tap into this amazing gift. I would recommend considering the following thoughts as you prepare people for altar leadership.

STEPS

1. Make the altar call clear. Explain this is for students who have not received the baptism in the Holy Spirit with the evidence of speaking in other tongues.
2. Bring people forward, but emphasize you are going to keep teaching so they don't "zone out" into their own prayer world.
3. Have the leaders/counselors come up behind them, but do not allow them to touch the students or begin to pray with them yet.
4. Explain the order of the altar time after everyone is in place. This order can include,
    a. Worship. This should continue until you feel the atmosphere is ripe to move on. Make sure you allow people to worship using their own words as well as songs.
    b. Have students ask Jesus for this gift of the baptism in the Holy Spirit. You can have them repeat a prayer after you or they can ask the Lord in their own words to baptize them in His Spirit with the evidence of speaking in other tongues.
    c. Have your leaders/counselors lay hands on the students and begin to pray in their own prayer language.
    d. Encourage students to speak their new language out loud.

Language
1. Begin with faith, not doubt. Encourage students that this can be their night to receive.
2. Explain the order of the altar time again.
3. Pray in your prayer language.
4. Dispel myths such as:
   a. You will feel something incredible.
   b. You are copying someone else's language.
   c. God will talk for you.
5. At the end of the altar service, remind those who did not receive that God loves them and encourage them to keep seeking.

Atmosphere
1. Create an atmosphere of anticipation.
2. Build faith.
3. Focus on this as an opportunity, not a burden.

General Thoughts
1. Encourage students to position themselves somehow in worship. Keep them engaged physically and their spirit will follow.
2. Tell them to focus on Jesus.
3. Be in it for the long haul. Some students receive quickly and others take awhile.
4. Don't be afraid to talk them through the process if they are struggling. Some need more teaching.

—Wayne Northup

The greatest encouragement I can give to students seeking the baptism in the Holy Spirit is to ask them if they trust Jesus with their life. Invariably they do, so I reaffirm that Jesus is the Baptizer and they just need to ask Jesus to reveal that part of himself to them.

A HEALTHY ENVIRONMENT FOR PREPARING VOLUNTEERS

How will you equip (Ephesians 4:11,12) the body to fulfill this work of the ministry? There are often more questions than answers concerning the specifics of how one is baptized in the Holy Spirit. Most pastors have received some type of training in the theological foundation of the Baptism but their volunteers may only have a personal experience to draw from. It shouldn't surprise us when volunteers have questions. Their belief can only be strengthened when questions can be asked, processed, embraced, and answered.

I suggest having a meeting or a series of meetings to provide teaching and allow time for questions far in advance of any preaching that will cover the Baptism and the altar call. In this way, leaders are more prepared and can present a more confident and faith-filled demeanor to the students they minister to at the altar. A ten-minute teaching before service begins does not provide adequate time for leaders to process questions, and it should not surprise us when that leader isn't as prepared for the altar service as we had hoped.

WORKING WITH DIFFERENT STUDENTS

Facilitating provides the environment, but there are also specific issues to address in the training and preparation of volunteers. Volunteer leaders will not only have a role at the altar time of a service but also have contact with the students outside of the service. These leaders need instruction on how to handle frustrated students, how to deal with "out of control" students, how to make appropriate physical contact, and how to guide students after the altar service.

It is very helpful to talk through scenarios that can occur during an altar time. I suggest being very specific about what you want and don't want to happen. For example, do you want the leadership team to come immediately to the front when the invitation is given to the students? Do you want some leaders to stay back? Whatever action you hope will take place, it is best if you communicate it ahead of time.

Frustrated students

Handling frustrated students at the altar is a common responsibility. You should let your volunteers know this can happen. Frustration has various causes. A student may have come forward many times before and is frustrated after waiting again through another altar time. Another student may be confused about what is happening around them. Friends might see something they are personally not experiencing and feel left out. Sometimes, insecurity can develop if a young person doesn't feel he or she is good enough to receive a gift from God. In all cases, it is usually best to take a break with the student. The leader should sit down and listen to the student, and then redirect his or her attention to the promises that were mentioned in the message.

"Out of control" students

Every volunteer leader needs to know what to do when unusual things happen. I served as a volunteer leader in a youth ministry while attending college. I vividly remember a prayer meeting where students were experiencing what has commonly been referred to as being "drunk in the Spirit." These students were laughing and stumbling around the room. I really do think God was touching these kids, but it was only five out of the eighty people in the room who were experiencing God in this way. At some point, the five "drunk" kids became a spectacle that was distracting the other seventy-five from praying. The advice of my youth pastor was poignant: "Take the kids out in the hall and pray with them. If it is real, they will experience the same thing without a crowd."

It is fairly common for spiritual activity to stir up expressions that have psychological origins. It is extremely important for a pastor to use discernment and address the appropriate action with either prayer or counseling. By training volunteers before they face certain scenarios, you can give them confidence to deal with the unknown.

Appropriate physical contact

Specific boundaries must be communicated in the area of physical contact. In most situations, prayer should be gender specific (males with males, females with females). Some basic boundaries should include placing a hand only on the shoulder, no rubbing or stroking of the back or neck, using discretion with hugging, and giving an absolute prohibition to being alone with a student. Finally, it may seem obvious, but in speaking of physical contact, breath mints are a good idea!

Taking it "to go"

The biggest challenge volunteer youth leaders face is helping students transition from a service experience into their everyday life. Students may have many questions about what this experience means for the rest of their life. It is similar to a fast food server asking, "Is this for here or to go?" Volunteer leaders need training in how to encourage students to take it "to go"—to live out the baptism in the Holy Spirit outside of church services.

I have a dream to see a new generation of pastors confidently inspiring the generations to whom they minister to "wait for the promise." This means new communication tools, experiences, and leaders will need to be developed and shared within the ministry family. May we never take this journey without the fulfillment of the promise of the Holy Spirit ourselves. May God grant you new wineskins as you lead the people God has called you to shepherd!

CHAPTER FOURTEEN

THEOLOGICAL, HISTORICAL, AND PRACTICAL INSIGHTS ON SPIRIT BAPTISM

By Dr. Gordon Anderson

I was saved as a young boy in a small Assemblies of God church, but I grew up in a former Assemblies of God church that was trying to distance itself from traditional Pentecostal baggage, the Latter Rain Movement in particular. This experience left me with the view that Pentecostals were emotional fanatics. Still, because of our Assemblies of God roots and family connections we visited some Pentecostal meetings.

I once went to a Latter Rain service with my parents. A.A. Allen was the speaker. I remember the end of the service when they were casting out demons. We were told to keep our eyes closed because when the demons came out they would look for a place to go, and would enter through the eyes of anyone watching. I closed my eyes, covered them with my hands, put my head down on my knees, and waited for all the demons to go away. That night reinforced my opinion of Pentecostals. We also visited an Assemblies of God summer camp meeting, which left me with mixed feelings at best. I can still remember the smell of the hamburgers being cooked for the after-service fellowship and I remember the joy all the people seemed to have. But the services were loud and long, very emotional, and didn't help me at all.

On the other hand, our family also attended an Oral

Roberts healing crusade. My grandmother had multiple sclerosis and was in a wheelchair. We all went forward with her for prayer. I was within just a few feet of Roberts, and must say I was deeply impressed with him. My grandmother was not healed, but my grandfather was, and with no prayer for him at all. He suffered terribly with arthritis, but was completely healed that night. The testimony of his healing was firmly entrenched in our family lore, and I didn't doubt it at all. This left me with an inner sense there was something very real to the supernatural work of the Holy Spirit.

Some years later my wife and I felt called into the ministry, attended an evangelical school to prepare, and turned up on staff in a charismatic church. I was hired to fill a part-time role before we ever attended a service. I did not know they were charismatic, and they did not know I was not. The details are too lengthy to tell, but suffice it to say, it was a strange mix.

I remember the first service, a Wednesday, where all my latent suspicions about Pentecostals were realized. The people jumped, waved their arms, clapped their hands, and danced in a unified aerobic-style jig. I didn't participate. Still, I knew they had something and I wanted it, even with all my questions. Four months later, after much study, prayer, and seeking, I was baptized in the Holy Spirit at home alone, a little after midnight. Later I joined the Assemblies of God, and have served in this Movement for some thirty-six years. Now I consider myself a traditional Pentecostal with some extra ideas planted along the way. I speak in tongues a lot, and believe the Baptism is indispensable.

The Bible says people receive power when the Holy Spirit comes upon them (Luke 24:49; Acts 1:8). But what really happens? The Bible uses a metaphorical picture to describe this event. It is called a "baptism," meaning an immersion. What does this mean? What actually happens when the Spirit comes on someone and they are baptized? A more technical description would indicate the Spirit initiates a new function or operation in a person's life when they are "baptized" and this new operation conveys power for ministry.

All Christians believe God forgives people and sanctifies their lives through the work of the Holy Spirit (who is God). This is called the salvific (salvation and sanctification) work of the Holy Spirit. Pentecostals believe there is more, where the Holy Spirit conveys power for ministry. This is the dynamic work. This event of having the Holy Spirit begin a new work, operation, or function is called a baptism.

This new work is a combination of divine (supernatural) power or energy and the operation or functioning of our human makeup. The Spirit comes on, flows through, and baptizes people. That is, the Spirit interacts with the human nature in such a way the person is able to be an agent of God's work. The Holy Spirit does something to people, and through them, to others.

This interaction of the divine and the human indicates people are somehow involved in the process. This involvement might be entirely passive, that is, they do absolutely nothing; or it might be active, that is, they do something to allow or cause this event to occur. This leads us in the direction of trying to discover just what people do, or can do, to facilitate this empowering experience.

A start at answering this question can be made by examining the biblical events where the Spirit baptized believers and listing what they were doing as part of this experience.

Luke 24:49: Jesus told the disciples to stay (wait) until they are clothed with power.

Acts 1:12 to 2:4: In the Upper Room the disciples were constantly praying (1:14); Peter spoke and conducted an election (1:16–26); they were all together (2:1); they were sitting (2:2).

Acts 8:14–17: Peter and John prayed for the people in the name of Jesus (vv. 15,16); they laid hands on them (v. 17); the people received the Holy Spirit (v. 17); Simon saw the Spirit was bestowed (v. 18).

Acts 9:1–19: Paul was on a journey to persecute believers (vv. 1,2); God did numerous things Paul did not initiate: a light appeared, he fell, heard a voice, was blinded, was led about, was prayed for, God talked to him, Ananias laid hands on him, he was healed (vv. 3–19).

Acts 10:26–48: Peter preached (vv. 28–43); the Spirit fell (v. 44); they spoke with tongues (v. 46); they were baptized in water (vv. 47,48).

Acts 19:1–7: Paul questioned and instructed the people (vv. 1–4); Paul baptized them in water (v. 5); Paul laid his hands on them (v. 6); the Spirit came upon them and they spoke with tongues (v. 6).

The key words and phrases indicating human activity include: stay, wait, constantly praying, speaking, election, all together, sitting, prayer in the name of Jesus, laying on of hands, journey, intent to persecute, preaching, questions, and instruction. In each case the people who received the Spirit were doing some of these things, but in no case did they do them all. This indicates some range of human action is part of the experience of receiving the Spirit—that there is variety, but no single pattern exists.

Interestingly, especially in Paul's case, God provided the initiative, worked against human will and intent, and provided the power to get him where God wanted him.

What else can we draw from these events? It seems other characteristics are part of these experiences as well. The disciples obeyed and went to the Upper Room, they were serious enough to wait for something they did not fully understand, they did know they were waiting for power for ministry, they were serious about the supernatural and ministry, they were ardent enough to press through to get answers to their questions, and at Caesarea they cooperated with things quite out of the norm (dreams, visions, cultural violations).

From all this we can conclude there are two primary ways the Spirit interacts with people to bring about a baptism in the Holy Spirit. First, illustrated in Paul's case, is where God provides all the initiative and the person is almost entirely passive. Second, there are times when people are engaged in a certain range of activities that seem to have some effect on the experience of being baptized in the Holy Spirit. We need not worry about the first process, illustrated by Paul's experience, since we can do nothing to start it (unless being an unregenerate persecutor of God's people is the key to initiating a call leading to the baptism in the Holy Spirit—a model we would not advocate). But we do recognize that in some cases the Baptism experience is entirely of God's doing.

It is the second case that interests us. There is a range of activity from which we can draw some insight into how people are baptized in the Holy Spirit. It is by following the example of these activities that we may properly create an atmosphere or participate in a process that leads to the baptism in the Holy Spirit.

If human activity were an intrinsic part of being baptized in the Spirit, then what kind of activity would it be? It must be the kind of activity that engages our human makeup in the process of having the Spirit of God begin a new operation or function of divine power in our lives. No single pattern can be drawn from the biblical incidents, but a general principle can be seen, and it is this: The various attributes, capacities, or human activities were surrendered to the power of the Spirit; that is, they were made available to, or were given over in a cooperative mode to the power of the Spirit with the intent the person in question would be empowered by God for supernatural purposes.

What are those human attributes or capacities? Human beings are made up of four main capacities or operations. They are the mind (intelligence, thinking, analysis, logic, knowledge), emotions (feelings, passion), will (obedience, rebellion, choice, volition, intention), and body (movement, activity, use of the various parts of the body). A review of the biblical examples cited earlier reveals in each case at least some of these characteristics were evident. Taking all the examples together, it seems all the elements of human makeup were engaged at one time or another. This should not be surprising.

Spiritual activity is the interaction of the characteristics and capacities of God with the characteristics and capacities of people. The Baptism is such an interaction and people will be successful in participating in this interaction, this Baptism, to the extent they are able to allow the various elements of their human makeup to interact with God. Leaders will be successful in helping people toward this end to the extent they can provide the kind of guidance, instruction, leadership, encouragement, and atmosphere to promote this process.

There are a number of different kinds of people in the world, but let's take a look at two that are rather different. First are the actional people. These people take initiative, jump in, act first and think later. They tend to be optimistic and have great faith. They also tend to be motivated by emotions. Peter is the model for this personality. The second are the analytical people. These people are slow to act, want to figure everything out first, are tentative and cautious. They tend to be more pessimistic and have trouble with faith. Thomas is the model for this personality.

Both have their strengths and weaknesses, neither is right or wrong, and neither is better than the other. Actional people have great starting power, but often lack staying power. Analytical people are very slow to start, but tend to keep going once they have made up their minds. This is instructive in considering how supernatural activity occurs in each of these personality types.

Actional people tend to respond well to high-energy, physically and emotionally engaging services. They respond well to altar services with a large group of people and a lot of activity and energy. Analytical people tend to hang back, watch and think (and criticize), do things on their own, and act alone. They do not respond well to altar services or following the lead of other people in working out their spiritual lives.

Again, this is not a matter of one being better or worse, of one being right or wrong. They are simply different. Since spiritual activity results from an interaction of the characteristics and capacities of God with the characteristics and capacities of people, then it should not be surprising that different kinds of activities and services help different kinds of people respond to God.

Traditional Pentecostals tend to fit primarily into the first category of people, the actional folks. This is especially true of early American Pentecostals.

So then, what can be done? How do you lead someone into the kind of activity that allows him or her to be baptized in the Holy Spirit? In addition to looking at the biblical examples, a review of historical examples is helpful. Pentecostals are all over the world and there is much variety among them, but two major groups can be identified and their practices are very revealing.

First are the traditional Pentecostals. They have their own unique practices. A typical event where people are baptized in the Holy Spirit could be called a camp meeting or revival atmosphere and usually involves the following: preaching about the Baptism, giving testimonies of the experience, altar, prayer, extended periods of waiting ("praying through"), a large group, a smaller group surrounding the seeker helping with a variety of activities ("praying them through to the Baptism"), loud and fast singing, laying on of hands, walking about (or even running and dancing), coaxing or urging ("let go, surrender to God, open up"), and praying in tongues so the seeker can hear. These activities engage the emotions and the body, but to a much lesser extent the mind and the will. These methods have proven to be very successful and a large percentage, perhaps a majority of traditional Pentecostals, testify this was their experience at a camp meeting, a summer youth camp, or some similar gathering.

I believe these activities are valid and a completely legitimate way of creating an atmosphere to help a seeker engage their human makeup with the supernatural power of God, resulting in a baptism in the Holy Spirit. However, I want to emphasize the range of human characteristics and capacities involved in all this is largely restricted to the emotional and physical dimensions. This is perfectly legitimate, and the results are valid. But this is not the only way for Baptism to occur.

A second group deserves attention. These are the charismatics. They are rather different from traditional Pentecostals and their methods of helping someone receive the Baptism are different as well. Among these people it is common for a service to be largely devoid of what has been described for traditional Pentecostals. The service or prayer time is quiet, the preaching is more of a teaching. The seeker may be sitting alone, or with one person who is there to help. The seeker is asked if they want the Holy Spirit and if they have asked for it. If they answer affirmatively, they are told they have it, because if we ask we receive, and God has promised He would give the Holy Spirit to those who ask.

Most charismatics, following the lead of Dennis Bennett, believe speaking in tongues is the evidence of receiving the Spirit, so the seeker is told to start speaking in tongues. The seeker then begins to make sounds resembling another language and is then told this is the outflow of the Holy Spirit and they should continue doing so until this ability becomes more common, more natural, and more fluid. The appeal here is to the mind and the will. I believe this method is legitimate.

I affirm the validity of these activities and believe they are a legitimate way of creating an atmosphere that helps a seeker engage their human makeup with the supernatural power of God, resulting in a baptism in the Holy Spirit. However, it is obvious the range of human characteristics and capacities involved are different than for traditional Pentecostals. Still, the charismatic movement has been very effective in helping people experience the baptism in the Holy Spirit.

Both of these ways are effective, but both have their problems. For traditional Pentecostals, doubts can arise after the experience. Not all have doubts, of course, but when they do arise they usually take the form of wondering if the emotional atmosphere resulted in a purely emotional response, and if all "help" provided by those in attendance created a coercive element where the expectation that the seeker would get something and do something was so great they were manipulated into the experience. This is especially true of those who have this experience in their youth, for example, at camp, where the emotional level and group pressure create a highly charged atmosphere.

Charismatics have their problems too. Again, not all have doubts, but the doubts that can arise in this camp take the form of wondering if the Holy Spirit really did conduct a baptism or if the seeker simply cooperated with a mimicking of tongues. The doubter wonders if it was all a product of human energy and activity, if the Holy Spirit had little to do with it, or if it was a legitimate Baptism regardless.

In more than thirty years of ministry I have heard many testimonies and talked with many people about their questions and doubts regarding Spirit baptism. It illustrates to me there is almost always enough human involvement present that the seeker can recognize the possibility that the human component was the controlling component. The exception to this is the Pauline example where God seems to have done it all, with no human effort and with no doubts afterward as well. I truly wish God would always do it this way, but when we consider the other biblical examples and the testimony of history, we find Paul's experience is more of a rarity.

I have had a number of Pauline experiences along the way, but my baptism in the Holy Spirit is not one of them. Mine was more of the charismatic type. I do not, however, have any doubts whatsoever that the Holy Spirit truly baptized me that night long ago and that power was conveyed to me for ministry. Through the years my dependence on the Holy Spirit and the practice of speaking in tongues has only grown as a major element in my own spiritual life.

Many traditional Pentecostals are having difficulty ministering to people and seeing them baptized in the Holy Spirit. As the Movement has matured, we have been giving emphasis to doctrines other than the Baptism. It used to be said that if you set a Pentecostal preacher's Bible on edge it would fall open to Acts 2:4. That is no longer the case. While we should preach and teach the whole counsel of God, we should not back away from a consistent presentation of our Pentecostal doctrines and practices.

The decline in the number of people who are being baptized in the Spirit causes a great deal of concern. The doctrine of speaking in tongues as evidence of the Baptism has been increasingly questioned. The teaching of delayed evidence which claims that speaking in tongues may follow the Baptism by a period of time has also surfaced. The regrettable result of this teaching is that some people claim to have been baptized in the Holy Spirit without speaking in tongues.

Following are a number of reasons why these issues have surfaced.

Experience without theology

The early leaders and proponents of the doctrine of the baptism in the Holy Spirit and the claim that this is attended by speaking in tongues at the same time had meaningful experiences, gave convincing testimonies, established movements, and conducted effective evangelistic and missionary ministries based on their Pentecostal convictions. But they did not write the kind of theology that could provide convincing intellectual and theological support for their claims. This is particularly noticeable as new evangelical leaders and movements have grown up making claims that the Baptism and speaking in tongues is not as important as Pentecostals have seen them to be. As a result, as questions have arisen, there is not a substantial body of theological writing to which people may turn to find answers.

Uncorrected abuses

Pentecostals have been reticent to correct people operating in the gifts of the Spirit because of their appreciation for the power of the Holy Spirit and their openness to allow things they do not fully understand or, more so, things with which they have a degree of discomfort. They fear "touching the anointed" too quickly. When abuses go unchecked, nonbelievers conclude Pentecostals are weird, at best, and crazy, at worst. In addition, young people in these churches may doubt the credibility of the whole thing. As they grow up, go into the ministry, or serve in local congregations, they are extremely cautious about allowing or promoting the operation of the gifts of the Spirit. They are not necessarily opposed, but they do not ardently pursue and promote these activities.

Moving from ardent promotion to amiable agreement

People do not contend ardently for those things about which they are not certain and passionate. Subsequent generations of Pentecostal leaders and people have diminished their support and promotion of Pentecostal activity, speaking in tongues in services, and supporting tongues as the initial evidence of the Baptism in particular. They still agree, but do not ardently promote. Amiable agreement without ardent promotion creates a climate of doubt, nonactivity, silence, and a decline in certitude and the frequency of these kinds of manifestations.

National Association of Evangelicals (1943)

The development of the National Association of Evangelicals (NAE) provided a place for like-minded Christians who saw themselves as neither fundamentalists nor liberals to identify together and share fellowship and ministry. The NAE was open to Pentecostals, and the Assemblies of God joined at the beginning, which was good. But, in their haste to be accepted by mainstream evangelical Christianity, some Pentecostals subordinated their Pentecostal identities and commitments to broader evangelical values. A debate emerged concerning Pentecostal identity, with some claiming Pentecostals are evangelicals first and Pentecostals afterward, seeing themselves as evangelicals who just happen to speak in tongues. Pentecostal practices and excesses tend to merge, with both pushed to the side in order to draw as little attention as possible to those things that might prove to be questionable or embarrassing. In this climate tongues and other Pentecostal values diminish. The NAE provided an opportunity for Pentecostals to join the mainstream, but with it another result has been seen, that of de-emphasizing Pentecostal values to gain acceptance and approval in evangelical circles.

Socioeconomic lift and increased sophistication

Pentecostals have moved from the "other side of the tracks" to the good neighborhoods and have built impressive buildings, quality educational institutions, sizeable organizations, and well-funded ministries. In the process, the values of first-generation pioneers have been superceded by those of more sophisticated successors. Pentecostals with roots that go back generations often speak affectionately about their predecessors even though there is precious little resemblance between the early leaders and their grandchildren. There is no outright criticism, mind you, but there is little imitation either. We have outgrown all that, it seems. These attitudes can be seen in the humorous stories told about the forefathers, the sweaty tabernacles and camps, healing and deliverance services, tarrying rooms, pioneer church planting, faith missions, and ramshackle schools, to name just a few.

Rise of the charismatic movement (1960)

Arising just seven years after the decline of the Latter Rain movement, Dennis Bennett and the charismatic renewal put speaking in tongues into the national spotlight. Along with this came a whole new set of ideas and practices that have had a significant impact on Pentecostal theology and practice. Much of this has been good, but within just a few years attention moved away from speaking in tongues as praise and worship gained in importance and prominence in services. Worship services took the place of Sunday School, Sunday evening services, and prayer meetings. In addition, the charismatics were committed to building up the existing church rather than adding to it through evangelism and missions. The movement produced no significant missions ministry. Since the primary purpose of the Baptism is to empower Christians for witness and service, diminished commitment to evangelism and missions also diminished the perceived need for the Baptism and for speaking in tongues as a function of supernatural empowerment. Over time, tongues became a prayer language, good for personal edification, with less emphasis on the miracle as a necessary part of witness and missions.

Rise of the Third Wave (1980)

Led by Fuller Seminary and key leaders (Wagner, Wimber, Kraft, and many others), the Third Wave movement ended the dominance of cessasionist theology, emphasized the role of signs and wonders in missions, and demonstrated the value and record of Pentecostal ministry. However, Third Wavers claimed the Baptism is part of salvation and that a subsequent experience, attended by speaking in tongues, is not necessary. The claim that people who do not speak in tongues may be used in signs and wonders created quite a problem for Pentecostals who, prior to 1980, could confidently assert the Baptism and speaking in tongues were necessary for the miraculous to occur in ministry. Lacking a compelling response to the Third Wave position, many joined Third Wave theology. The result is that the importance and necessity of being baptized in the Holy Spirit and speaking tongues has been questioned, denied, and diminished by some.

Rise of Evangelical "stars"

The ministries of Billy Graham, Bill Bright, Chuck Swindoll, Charles Stanley, Bill Hybels, and Rick Warren have raised the question of the necessity of being Pentecostal. None of these are Pentecostal, or even charismatic or Third Wave, for that matter.

With this in view, is the Baptism really an important, needed, subsequent event, evidenced by speaking in tongues? Pentecostals have not yet given an answer that convinces many who are impressed by these ministries and the theology that lies behind them.

Diminished growth in the U.S. Assemblies of God

If the ethnic growth in the Assemblies of God is removed, the statistics are unimpressive, giving rise to serious questions. Some wonder how correct, important, and necessary traditional Pentecostal doctrines and practices are in light of the growth statistics.

Confused Pentecostal theology

Pentecostals have long claimed their distinctive doctrine is speaking in tongues, but this may have been a misplaced emphasis that is now creating serious problems. This claim can have the effect of making Pentecost all about speaking in tongues, other more important issues getting lost. Emphasizing tongues is a unique feature of Pentecostals. Speaking in tongues is a necessary part of being baptized in the Holy Spirit, but it is not the heart. The core purpose of the Baptism is power for supernatural ministry. Consider this; Pentecostals believe, along with Paul, that signs and wonders are an intrinsic part of evangelism and church planting (1 Corinthians 2:1–5). However, at the same time, Pentecostals use non-Pentecostals to teach church planting, with the role of signs and wonders largely if not entirely absent from the curriculum. Pentecostal leaders might ask potential church planters if they are Pentecostal and if they speak in tongues; good and important questions, but perhaps it would be better to discover if they have the ability to preach the Word to nonbelievers with attending signs and wonders. Is it speaking in tongues or supernatural ministry that truly makes Pentecostals unique?

Relegation of the baptism in the Holy Spirit to camps and other special gatherings

Many Pentecostal churches rarely have services and prayer meetings where the Baptism is emphasized and where opportunity to receive the Spirit is given. Instead, this is accomplished primarily through the ministry of camps or seminars, or the specialized emphasis of an itinerant minister. Pastors and churches do not include this practice as a mainstay in the church life as much as we did earlier in our history. If we take the youth camp program out of our activities, the number of people who can claim to have been baptized in the Holy Spirit will diminish dramatically.

Pentecostals now face a number of issues that must be addressed adequately if we are to continue to provide leadership to the rest of the church world with regard to Pentecostal ministry. Church statistics tell us the twenty-first century is a Pentecostal century. Around the world Pentecostal ministry is leading the way. It is in North America that the questions are emerging and the Pentecostals are lagging. The issues outlined in this lesson need to be addressed. My prayer is that we Pentecostals will rise to the challenge of providing answers to legitimate questions and that we may be able to articulate with passion and conviction a theology of the Spirit that the church needs in order to preach the Kingdom and plant the church in our present world.

Traditional American Pentecostals have changed over the years and the methods used earlier in our history will not be successful now in every situation. We have more analytical and fewer actional types, by and large, in our churches today. Many leaders find it impossible to use methods of the past to help seekers in the present. This is not uniformly the case, but it is much more frequent than ever before. Most of our churches do not follow a camp meeting style of services. Besides that, most of our leaders (pastors and musicians) could not create a camp meeting or revival atmosphere if they had to. The style of preaching and music from that era is largely gone.

Some think the key to Pentecostal theology and practice is to continue the leadership styles of previous decades, and that to do otherwise compromises the reality of the experience of the Baptism. Others, knowing it would be a disaster to try to introduce these methods into today's congregations, have given up, not knowing how to lead today's people into the Baptism. Still others, reticent to admit leaders really do create an environment to facilitate spiritual activity, have adopted the Pauline model by default.

"If God wants to do it, He can. But we won't do anything that leaves us vulnerable to the charge we are manipulating people and coercing them into a spiritual experience." Moreover, we tend to describe the leadership methods of the past in terms of Paul's divine arrest, obliterating the fact we really did know how to lead, facilitate, and create an atmosphere to help people into spiritual experiences.

CONCLUSION

What then should we do? I believe Pentecostal leaders must take a very proactive approach to helping people experience the baptism in the Holy Spirit. We should determine the approach we need to take to create an atmosphere that facilitates this vital dimension of spirituality, one that will be effective in our own situation. We need to ensure the human activities we choose to implement are appropriate and legitimate, and recognize that to utilize them energetically is valid and essential. In any event and in every case we must find ways to help people get through to the baptism in the Holy Spirit. It is indispensable.

CHAPTER FIFTEEN

A LINGUIST LOOKS AT THE MYSTERY OF TONGUES

By Dr. Del Tarr

Tongues is God's joke on human reason.
—ISAAC CANALES

An unprecedented spiritual renewal has swept the world in the last one hundred years. As late as the mid-twentieth century—fifty years into this move of God—almost no one anticipated it would be called by some the "Century of the Pentecostals." At this writing at least 650 million living believers practice, or at least subscribe to the doctrinal position of speaking in tongues (glossolalia). "Statisticians tell us that more than 1.5 billion people associate themselves with this global revival movement."[1]

Pentecostals are now the second-largest theological segment of Christianity—second only to the Roman Catholic Church (who themselves count over seventy-five million charismatics among their number).[2] Early Pentecostals moved from what was considered normal in church circles concerning the role the Holy Spirit plays in church and personal life, to that which was considered abnormal by the churches they were a part of when they experienced the Baptism in the Holy Spirit. For this experience many paid the high price of expulsion from their traditional denominations.

Pentecostals are not meant to be "mainstream." God help us if we ever get there. We have made great social strides from the tent revivals and storefront churches of the past, which may be good. But if God doesn't show up in our robed choirs, tuned orchestras, and timed services, we will have left God's biblical pattern—which some may perceive as foolish—and become another run-of-the-mill clergy-dominated organization.

I hope to stimulate new thinking by a somewhat unorthodox look at an issue that is baffling to so many—speaking in tongues. How could one-fourth of all Christendom today be made up of these "tongue-talkers'? How could their numbers have grown so fast in the space of one hundred years? The kingdom of God, as announced by Jesus, was seen as unorthodox in the midst of Jewish culture in the first century. God's kingdom—as seen through the lens of secular (and even some religious) circles—still seems to be an anomaly. Yet as witnesses and communicators we must face the dilemma, accept the ambiguous "upside-down"[3] nature of the gospel, resist the attempt to make it "reasonable," yet still present it as relevant. Does that sound antithetical—even impossible? I would assert that an effective communicator of the gospel today must make the language understood to his immediate audience, allowing how "unreasonable" the gospel is, while still showing how desperately it remains mankind's only hope for life, happiness, and future security.

Although we think by using words we are only communicating one message, in reality we are communicating many more. We think we are communicating only ideas, but by facial expressions, gestures, tone of voice, body posture, the distance between people, use of time, and other factors, we are communicating feelings, values (such as distrust, concern, disdain, agreement, etc.), and more. A person usually recalls these even more vividly than the words themselves!

NO ONE PRACTICES GOOD COMMUNICATION NATURALLY

We have to work very hard to communicate well, and even then misunderstandings still occur. We utilize words of our own thinking to which we have "fixed meanings" representing the way we internalize them. These assigned "meanings" were only assigned for ourselves—not the people to whom we direct these messages. And we unreasonably expect them to *decode* them the way we *encoded* them.

The process of becoming is contingent upon seeing the other person's point of view and *encoding* a message into his or her perceptual field. Even though He made humans with a capacity for interpersonal communications superior to animals, God knows that good communication is hard for us. So, He sent His Son Jesus to explain (encode) His message into our "database" of information. Since humans don't understand God's database easily, He adopted ours! This is the great wonder of the Incarnation of Christ. The great wonder of "God with us" is God's willingness to accommodate himself, to come to our level; in turn, Jesus made himself easier to be understood. He was born a Jewish baby and grew up in human form to *encode* God's message into the world of His hearers! (Philippians 2:5–11) God loved us that much!

ATTENTION! DANGER AHEAD!

Understanding the nature of communication is important to better understand why glossolalia seems so foolish for some people, especially Western man. This great gift to mankind of communication prowess is from God himself, but in the hands of fallen mankind, it can be distorted to be man's potent enemy, keeping us from the very intention of the Creator who gave it so we could have interpersonal relations with Him. This is related to how proud humans are about their ability to make meaning with words. We are at the top of the communication chain of all God's creatures. We have designated the human intellect to be supreme. It's our most prideful accomplishment and many of the top jobs and positions in commerce, the arts, and even the religious world go to those who master speech.

In addition to that, written speech (literature) is now the standard of the whole educational system. But in God's ultimate wisdom, He knew of carnal man's temptation to use the gift of speaking and writing as a weapon of pride. Print literacy has become both man's ultimate tool of intellectual advancement, and also the tool of his self-deception through pride. The Rationalization of the faith and Protestant Scholasticism make a written text more important that its author—even the author of the Bible. "Textualization" alienates Christian people from the *oral* nature of much of God's intention of interaction with us. Guttenberg's printing press which helped bring about the Great Reformation and forever changed the Western world has given us a five hundred year "print bias" of which we are largely unaware.[4] We have a built-in resistance to God's prophetic intention as evidenced in the New Testament.

Are not those who would refuse to consider the baptism in the Holy Spirit, or deny its effectiveness also denying the limitations of human speech? Is not this a renewal of a scholasticism of an earlier age?

Here lies one of the problems with tongues and prophecy and other gifts—they are not literate! They are oral expressions in communication under the inspiration of the Holy Spirit. A modern society fixated on literacy has great difficulty accepting their legitimacy. A literate society encourages rational thought even at the expense of feelings; in fact, feelings are generally seen as suspect and should be divorced from ideas.

Tongues cannot be written down, systematized, or repeated. Like the manna of the Old Testament, that could not be stored, a "new" infusion is always needed! It cannot be predicted or put in a church bulletin or litany. So, tongues are perceived as dangerous! The apostle Paul says that when speaking in tongues, the mind is "unfruitful" (1 Corinthians 14:14) and tongues are often related to feelings. Biblically, glossolalia must be controlled by the community and its leaders. Sadly, those same leaders, in turn, often fear God's "inbreaking" unless that event can be scheduled! Glossolalia has been marginalized or prohibited by the ultra "literate" conservative modern Pharisees who have completely internalized words like "inerrant," "authorized," or "systematized." All those concepts are good in correct context, but when overemphasized in the context of the Holy Spirit, they quench the Spirit. Paul the apostle said "Do not put out the Spirit's fire" (1 Thessalonians 5:19). Interesting, this "fire" metaphor and how often it is repeated in the New Testament.

Pentecostals and charismatics believe the renewal of the gifts of the Spirit in religious worship and mission is a return to the oral character of the original New Testament model. Most Pentecostals in the early twentieth century were hoping to help renew the churches where they already worshipped (like Martin Luther had hoped to do in the Roman Church), but instead were rejected and put out of the community. One must ask: How much of their rejection is related to the same rejection and marginalization by traditional "literate and linear" Christian communities now? Where only written creeds, liturgy, and litanies are trusted, people are quick to reject oral and spontaneous-oriented worship.

A PLEA TO RE-EXAMINE

No one would question the value of communication in written form where it can be stored, compared unchanged after hundreds of years, while oral communication can quite easily be redefined or shifted in content. Literacy is extremely valuable—we can't go back. But we can examine what it has done to a valuable form of human communication still used by the majority of the world's peoples. And we might look at how our literary predisposition may have produced a built-in bias against spontaneous prayer language as found in Acts 2, 9, 11 and 1 Corinthians 12 through 14, plus many other accounts in the New Testament record.

UPSIDE-DOWN WISDOM

The apostle Paul, the writer in the New Testament responsible for more books than any other, makes a definitive contribution to this issue by writing to the new Christians in the Roman city of Corinth. This city was known for its commerce, its vice, and its love of wisdom (*sophia*) from the Greeks. The apostle was criticized by the Sophists in the congregation for not speaking sophisticated enough for their fine minds. Here are his words in defense of his choice of communication style: "Christ did not send me to baptize, but to preach the gospel—not with words of human wisdom, lest the cross of Christ be emptied of its power" (1 Corinthians 1:17). Gordon Fee says that almost certainly all the language in this passage having to do with eloquence and persuasive words is also related to this theme.[5] The wisdom of speech, encoding from a superior rhetorical skill, chooses eloquent self-attracting complicated words that demonstrate excellency so admired by a few intellectuals who like to denigrate the unlearned. But, in so doing, they empty the Cross of its power. How is that? Because the message of the cross of Christ is upside-down with the world's wisdom and logic. Paul rejects wisdom (*sophia*) as a rhetorical device because in its presentation it overshadows the essence of the whole plan of the universe which makes an upside-down, impossible "joke" (in the eyes of the worldly wise) of Christ's death. Man's database of knowledge, past experience, values, attitudes, etc. makes the Cross look like a foolish error.

In like manner, hyper-linearity and literalism—the mastery of reason and analysis—the intimidating force of skillful oratory that makes an icon of human speech skills, would displace the role of the Holy Spirit who seeks, through glossolalia, to make human weakness miraculously strong in an act of perceived foolishness, so the true power of the Cross may have preeminence in salvation as well as discipleship and servanthood.

Pentecostals or charismatics are not better people or better communicators naturally, but they have learned and experienced—through tongues speech—the submission of their own mental and verbal skills to the Holy Spirit. Thus, they have been empowered to believe (greatly enhancing their courage) that God wants them to be useful vessels, as humble servants, for the proclamation of His gospel. Added to this is the fact that speaking in tongues (as the initial physical evidence of Jesus' words in Acts 1:5, "John baptized with water, but in a few days you will be baptized with the Holy Spirit.") is like a new door through which the recipient can believe God and seek other gifts of the Spirit such as faith, miracles, prophecy, healings, word of wisdom and knowledge. These are not signs of holiness but tools to work in the field to produce fruit.

This does not mean that non-Pentecostals are inferior witnesses. History proves they can be very powerful witnesses. My contention is that they can be even more effective after having been "clothed" by the mighty baptism of the Holy Spirit.

Just like God hid the power of the Cross behind its apparent foolishness, so He has hidden the power of the Holy Spirit for the most effective witness behind the symbol of total submission and the "foolishness" of glossolalia! God chose the foolishness of the Cross (a Messiah killed in an ignominious death) to redeem us. I submit, He chose the foolishness of tongues as the symbol, the required "getting lost" enough, to empower us for witness so we'd be motivated to lose our lives to find them (Matthew 10:39).

This is why tongues is no doubt the superior sign (given in Acts 2, 10, 19) over any of the other gifts of the Spirit (listed in Romans 12; 1 Corinthians 12, 14; Ephesians 4) that glossolalia is not self-created! Why not prophecy? Is this good? Yes, of course. Do we need it? Yes, Paul makes it clear, we need prophecy, and in some contexts it is even more desirable. Why not the word of wisdom or word of knowledge as signs to the individual the Spirit is resident? Because those gifts of the Spirit operate in the medium of the "understood language" of both the hearers and the speaker of the gift. The user of any of those gifts may always doubt part or the whole of its source as being supernatural because the human mind is active in selecting and sorting with proper syntax and sentence structure for the sake of cognition (conscious thought). The "spirit within him—man's own spirit" knows that he or she is not the source of glossolalia, if it is genuine. It cannot be memorized. It cannot be just gibberish, or made up to impress or trick. The "thoughts of a man know this." And when it is genuine, a person also knows this deep within, contrary to the element of doubt that can exist when a spiritual gift operates in a person's known language.

Our cessationist and doubting spiritual siblings in the body of Christ are certainly right to compare this powerful truth to Romans 8:16 ("The Spirit himself testifies with our spirit that we are God's children"), but they don't have the capacity, through their own choosing or ignorance—like a veil—to see this does not only concern salvation. But in the context of a New Testament charismatic church where glossolalia was normal and everywhere pervasive, this passage also speaks to the charismatic world of the building up of the confidence of the speaker. In private prayer and intercession or in public edification of the worshipping believing church, the believer comes to know he or she can be the Lord's instrument to fulfill the Ascension mandate of Acts 1:8 (to be His witnesses).

No man would have chosen glossolalia—any more than any Jew would have chosen a Messiah to appear to be so weak to let himself get killed by the ignominious death of the Roman cross.

It's idolatry to make a system of salvation that omits God's plan of the Cross. Man says: "If I'm to believe in you, you must do it my way, in a way that's less costly, in a way whereby I can merit or earn my way. I refuse to be beholden; I'll accept no grace." So it's also idolatrous to say: "I will have the fullness of the Holy Spirit—but on my terms. And my terms will omit any foolishness and especially any stigma such as 'these men are drunk'" (Acts 2:13). By insisting on tongues, God insured that man, in his pride, would stumble over the true source of power that only comes by submission and weakness.

Those who say "God is reasonable" must be reading a different version of the Bible than I read. God is a God of risk. God even risks a partnership with humanity, as unreasonable as that may seem. He doesn't *need* to do this—He *wants* to do this. By allowing a believer to be the delivery system of the gifts of the Spirit (and especially the vocal gifts), God is taking a chance with us. Down through the ages, the Church has wanted to help God out and eliminate the chance of human error. That thought has now invaded many of those who profess to be Pentecostal.

Has God chosen what seems foolish so that the wrong people miss His bounty? Is this seemingly "foolishness" God's filter?

NO ROOM FOR THE FANATIC

True, there is absolutely no room for fanaticism and abject carnality as is sometimes seen in the ranks of professing people of the Spirit. They embarrass us all. But the church must not make the mistake some make with a fireplace. Instead of using the tongs for an occasional coal that jumps out onto the hearth and throwing it back where it belongs (this is the control of the gifts by the body of Christ, as in Paul's admonition), they reach for the other tool next to the fireplace—the extinguisher! All that's left are cold, wet ashes. Let us, instead, trust the Holy Spirit to find the balance between dead orthodoxy and the words of Paul to the Thessalonians, "Do not put out the Spirit's fire!" (1 Thessalonians 5:19).

1. Thomas Trask, "Pentecost: Empowerment for Life-Changing Ministry," *Enrichment* 10 (Winter 2005): 144.

2. John Radano, director Pontifical Council for Promoting Christian Unity, personal interview with author in Rome, Italy, 1998.

3. One of the best sources in the area of upside-down thinking is a recent book by Ernest B. Gentile, *The Glorious Disturbance* (2004).

4. At the turn of the century, the History Channel surveyed many historians and made a list of the one hundred most influential people in the past one thousand years. Interestingly, Gutenberg was listed as number one.

5. Gordon D. Fee and C. K. Barrett, *Corinthians: A Study Guide*, Brussels, Belgium: International Correspondence Institute, 1979.